SEX AND SEXUALITY

Winnicott Studies Monograph Series

The Person Who Is Me:
Contemporary Perspectives on the True and False Self
edited by Val Richards

Fathers, Families, and the Outside World
edited by Val Richards

André Green at The *Squiggle Foundation*
edited by Jan Abram

Art, Creativity, Living
edited by Lesley Caldwell

The Elusive Child
edited by Lesley Caldwell

The *Squiggle* Foundation is a registered charity
set up in 1981 to study and cultivate the tradition
of D. W. Winnicott. For further information, contact
The Administrator, 33 Amberley Road, London N13 4BH.
Tel: 020 8882 9744; Fax: 020 8886 2418

Winnicott Studies Monograph Series

SEX AND SEXUALITY
Winnicottian Perpectives

edited by
Lesley Caldwell

KARNAC

LONDON   NEW YORK

for
The *Squiggle* Foundation

Extract on pp. 60–61 by Phyllis Greenacre reprinted from "The Primal Scene and the Sense of Reality", in *The Psychoanalytic Quarterly*, Vo. 42, No. 1 (1973): pp. 10–41. Copyright © The Psychoanalytic Quarterly, 1973.

Poem on p. 121, "maggie and milly and molly and may", is reprinted from *Complete Poems 1904–1962* by E. E. Cummings, edited by George J. Firmage, by permission of W. W. Norton & Company. Copyright © 1991 by the Trustees for the E. E. Cummings Trust and George James Firmage.

Extracts in chapter 6 from D. W. Winnicott, *Human Nature* (1988, pp. 59, 36, 99, 100), *The Piggle* (1977, p. 158), *Didactic Statement on Child Development* (unpublished), and *Playing and Reality* (1971, pp. 2, 65, 223–224) reprinted by permission of Paterson Marsh Ltd. on behalf of The Winnicott Trust.

Extracts in chapter 7 from *Orpheus, Eurydice, Hermes* from *Selected Works Volume II* by Rainer Maria Rilke and translated by J. B. Leishman and published by The Hogarth Press. Used by permission of St John's College, Oxford and The Random House Group Limited, and of Suhrkamp Verlag.

First published in 2005 by
H. Karnac (Books) Ltd.
6 Pembroke Buildings, London NW10 6RE

British Library Cataloguing in Publication Data

A C.I.P. for this book is available from the British Library

ISBN: 1-85575-909-8

10 9 8 7 6 5 4 3 2 1

Edited, designed, and produced by Communication Crafts

Printed in Great Britain

www.karnacbooks.com

CONTENTS

v

CONTRIBUTORS

MARIO BERTOLINI is a training analyst of the Italian Psychoanalytical Association (AIPsi). He is full Professor of Child Neuropsychiatry and Director of the Winnicottian Studies Programme at the University of Milano-Bicocca, Faculty of Medicine. He is editor of *Squiggles and Space* (2001).

LESLEY CALDWELL is the editor of the Winnicott Studies Monograph Series and an editor of the Winnicott Trust. From 2000 to 2003 she was director of the Squiggle Foundation. She is a Visiting Fellow in the Department of Italian at University College London and works as a psychoanalytic psychotherapist in private practice.

ANDREAS GIANNAKOULAS is a full member and training analyst of the AIPsi and of the British Psychoanalytical Society.

ANDRÉ GREEN is a training analyst of the Paris Psychoanalytic Society and an Honorary Member of the British Psychoanalytical Society. He is a Patron of The *Squiggle* Foundation.

JOYCE MCDOUGALL, D.Ed., is supervisory and training analyst to the Paris Psychoanalytic Society and Institute, honorary member of the

Association for Psychoanalytic Medicine (New York), member of the New York Freudian Society, and on the teaching staff of the Object Relations Institute, New York. She is the author of *Plea for a Measure of Abnormality*, *Theatres of the Mind*; *Theatres of the Body*, and *The Many Faces of Eros* and co-author of *Dialogue with Sammy*. She is a Patron of The *Squiggle* Foundation and is in private practice.

FRANCESCA NERI is an analyst of AIPsi and Professor of Child Neuropsychiatry at the Faculty of Medicine, University of Brescia.

ADAM PHILLIPS was formerly Principal Child Psychotherapist at Charing Cross Hospital, London. He is a Patron of The *Squiggle* Foundation.

HELEN TAYLOR ROBINSON is a full member of the British Psychoanalytical Society and is in full-time private practice. She is a Trustee for the Winnicott Trust and co-edited *Thinking about Children* (1996). She was formerly Honorary Senior Lecturer at University College London, where she taught on the Master's in Theoretical Psychoanalysis.

DOMINIQUE SCARFONE, a psychiatrist and psychoanalyst, is a member of the Canadian Psychoanalytic Society (Montreal French branch) and of the Canadian Psychoanalytic Institute. He is Professor in the Department of Psychology, Université de Montréal.

MAGGIE SCHAEDEL is a Consultant Adult Psychotherapist in the National Health Service where she is developing a new service for survivors of sexual abuse. She holds a lectureship in Psychoanalytic Psychotherapy at the University of Kent and is in private practice.

SEX AND SEXUALITY

CHAPTER ONE

Introduction

Lesley Caldwell

Despite Winnicott's statement in his posthumously published *Human Nature* (1988) that "Any theory that bypasses the importance of instinct and the significance of childhood sexuality is unhelpful" (p. 36), the impact of sexual difference and its organization of human individuality, the place of the drives, and the dominance of sexuality so central to the Freudian schema are not usually understood as forming an integral part of Winnicott's concerns.

His account of human development makes fundamental the environmental provision that originates in the actual relations between mother and baby and gives considerable weight to physiological changes as part of the conditions for the emergence of an incipient psychic structure. This privileges the body and its handling in the acquisition of all the capacities of being human and makes maternal care and the body fundamental to the development of mental functioning. Without losing sight of the more familiar preoccupations associated with Winnicott, the articles collected in this volume present an account that is attentive to sexuality—particularly infantile sexuality—and they explore a Winnicott

1

unapologetically linked to Freud and to a psychoanalysis located in the drives. The volume offers a less familiar approach to Winnicott's work, and in so doing it invites a different engagement with the traditional concerns of British psychoanalysis.

"In terms of baby and mother's breast (I am not claiming that the breast is essential as a vehicle of mother-love) the baby has instinctual urges and predatory ideas. The mother has a breast and the power to produce milk, and the idea that she would like to be attacked by a hungry baby" (1945, p. 152). This matter-of-fact assertion of the essential ambivalence at the heart of the feeding relationship—of how, through the propping of the drive upon need, "infantile sexuality attaches itself to one of the vital somatic functions" (Freud, 1905d, p. 182)—describes the mother–child relationship in terms of reciprocal desire and the coexistence of aggression and sexuality for what Winnicott calls the "excited" infant. But his paper does not elaborate on the potential relationships for both participants assumed by such a description, nor does it develop, as did Ferenczi earlier and Laplanche later, the basis of the mother's desire or the seduction signified by her availability. Instead, it uses the link between early life and later disturbance to think about the place of infantile fantasies and when and how they may be said to develop. There is a strongly contemporary feel both to this concern with the baby's realizations about the world and about him/herself and to the different kinds of analyses demanded by different patients. Winnicott proposes that this demand originates in patients' fantasies about two separate, but related things: about the analyst and what she or he is doing and why, and about the self and what happens inside it. Each involves sexuality and the links between psychic and physiological growth in acceding to the attributes of being human. Each calls up the necessity of the other in the establishment of human subjectivity and how this is to be thought about and engaged with in the arena delimited by psychoanalysis.

Winnicott's interest in the emotional and psychological implications of the shift that occurs in babies around age 5 to 6 months leads him to infer that a fundamental human achievement—the localization of the self in a body—together with the growing recognition of existing in time and space, become established as the baby moves from being unintegrated to a state of integration through external, usually maternal, care and its psychic consequences.

Infantile sexuality is certainly significant, but only after this move from unintegration to integration has been effected and the baby comes to a realization of a world outside itself and the limits imposed by that world on the world of unlimited fantasy that preceded it. To ask when and how emotional responses register, and how such a registration is to be conceptualized, is to pursue a different set of questions from those of Freud or Klein. Indeed, what Winnicott stresses is not loss and depression in the face of progressive disillusion, but the advantages of a realization that what can be imagined has its limits. He proposes that what might be at stake in the idea that a baby's need *is* met, and how the baby may register such a moment in fantasy, relates to the baby's desire, but the desire has different components. While acknowledging the strength of a baby's wishes, Winnicott sees the tasks confronting the infant in sustaining his or her instinctual experiences as second-ary to negotiating the existence of a self that can take on that negotiation. This amounts to a divergence about the origins and the form of human individuality and difficulty, but, rather than being a rejection of the Freudian schema, it may be seen as a revision based upon the evidence of close continuing observation, com-bined with a willingness to speculate convincingly about what is observed. Both "Primitive Emotional Development" (1945) and "The Observation of Infants in a Set Situation" (1941) argue for an analytic and paediatric interest in the interrelation of body, mind, and psyche by hypothesizing about the probable psychological referents that accompany or produce minute shifts in physiological arousal in the infant. Winnicott's extensive interest in the somatic indicators of psychic states, and his elaboration of how the infant becomes a human being, is an intensive study of the *conditions without which* the drives can never be accommodated sufficiently for the subject to begin to live a normal life (with all of the abnor-mal, psychoanalytically speaking, which that entails).

What mainly followed from these concerns was a form of theo-rizing predominantly interested in the implication for later health of early infantile states. These interests place Winnicott, and the originality of his attempts to describe the formation of the self, in a solidly English tradition of psychoanalytic work and thought. At the same time, his way of writing is an intensely idiosyncratic challenge to some of its more pragmatic priorities. Eric Rayner's

(1991) account of the Independent group identifies the appeal of a particular way of going about things for the group of whom Winnicott was a leading member, an appeal that formed part of a more general English approach where the impact of internal configurations on early development and a comprehensive turn to object relations displaced Freud's account of sexuality and the drives as the basis of human subjectivity. Susan Budd (2001) has provided a useful historical account of British psychoanalysis and its involvement in that specific tendency of "Englishness" which is discomforted by intellectuals and by intellectual activity. How those cultural roots helped shape the actual interests and working methods that came to distinguish British psychoanalysis is of interest not only for Winnicott but for the other distinguished clinicians of the British school. What emerges of his choices in the consulting-room, particularly with adult patients, choices certainly shared by most of his colleagues in the postwar period, seems to propose something else: a sexuality that is both there and not there, assumed and demonstrated, displaced and concealed.

This can be seen in the account of some of the work from a long analysis with a female patient reported in the late paper, "Dreaming, Fantasying, and Living" (1971a). There he discusses the differences between dreaming and fantasying in terms of the former's creative associations with living, and the latter's representation of a state of non-living, a pursuit of mental stasis, of non-activity, which he describes as "dissociated". He reports two dreams brought by the patient that deal with the theme of having and producing a child. The dreams in themselves reveal how far a part of the patient has moved from fantasying to the living and engaged activity that is dreaming, and Winnicott summarizes for himself, for the patient, and for the reader what the distinction between them entails. He does not emphasize what could be thought of as the *libidinally invested aspects* of this fantasying, this activity aimed at non-activity, this "fantasying" as it appears in the therapeutic relationship in the session. The patient's instinctual urges themselves appear to be left "formless," in the sense that they are not given form *verbally* in Winnicott's interpretations. This absence is particularly marked because of the manifest content of the dreams, and the associations that are reported as emerging in the analytic work. The patient's belief that she has a girl child of about 10 is recognized and made explicit; the existence of a man who is the child's father appears, and so does her mother, who is seen as depriving her of children. The patient is able to say, "The funny thing is that here I look as if I am wanting a child, whereas in my conscious thought I know that I only think of children as needing protection from being born" (pp. 30–31).

In the next session the patient begins by returning to what the analyst had said about fantasying as interfering with dreaming: "I woke at midnight and there I was hectically cutting out, planning, working on the pattern for a dress. I was all but doing it and was het up. Is that dreaming or fantasying? I became aware of what it was all about but I was awake" (p. 32). There is the immediate challenge this woman is making to her analyst and his accounts are reported without comment, but Winnicott describes how they continue to talk around the subject with a striking use of words: "working herself up in this way restricts her from action". The patient responds by describing how she listens to talks on the radio while playing patience. Winnicott interprets again and then provides an example of her doing a similar thing *"at that moment"* (my italics) in the session: "while I was talking she was fiddling with the zip of her bag: why was it this end? how awkward it was to do up! She could feel that this dissociated activity was more important to her sitting there than listening to what I was saying" (p. 32).

In the exchange that follows, the patient describes going off yet again, and the Winnicott reports: "here again . . . she felt dissociated as if she could not be in her skin" (p. 32). Although he goes on to talk of her *bodily* involvement as producing great tension and a lack of psychosomatic climax, as it is recorded here he does not connect this or the symptomatic act with the zip to any sexualized dimension. The resonance with Dora (Freud, 1905d) and her reticule seems to emphasize the possible sexual associations. Freud links Dora's vaginal discharge with her mother and her unconscious wish to be like her mother—that is, to have also been infected by her father's venereal disease. So he proposes that Dora's masturbation has a part in her neurosis, and she flatly denies it. But, a few days later, she is wearing a little reticule, "and as she lay on the couch she kept playing with it—opening it, putting a finger into it, shutting it again and so on". Freud robustly goes on to give Dora a lesson in symptomatic acts, a more outspoken version of Winnicott's explanations of fantasying and dreaming to his patient, whose attempt to make what her analyst says foolish and contemptuous—"So that's what *you* think" (p. 32)—also contains echoes of Dora.

The wish for a frozen moment would seem to be directed at subverting the unconscious transference implications contained in the diachronic dimension of the session, and Winnicott adds that the patient recognizes the paralysis of action that is the aim of this fantasying. My interest here is in his decision not to take up the possible transference aspects of how his patient's recourse to an essentially substitutive activity (taken to a level he describes as "dissociated") may enact what could be at stake in an absence of sexual activity and its implications. Something seems to be left out, and that something is, or could be, the transference dimensions of sexuality and its organization of the patient's material. This is not to maintain that what is taken up and reported is any less appropriate or less "correct" than an interpretation that confronted the transference currency of sexual fantasy. Rather, it is to suggest that choices about the level at which to interpret, about oedipality, and about sexuality and aggression relate not only to the patient but also to the analyst's personality and to the culture of which that analyst is a part. Any extended account of this fascinating area would need to address how theoretical commitments and preferences, or adhesion to particular psychoanalytic schools and preferred ways of working, are necessarily linked with psychic structure and psychic choices. (Roustang, 1982; Spurling, 2002).

One of Winnicott's starting points is the link between the physical body and the infant's instinctual impulses, the interrelation of psyche and soma from the beginning; however, in some of the work with adults the sexuality of the patient, of the analyst, and of the analytic relationship seems to disappear. For the contributors in this volume, sexuality is central, and what is interesting about Winnicott's ideas is their contribution to this orientation. This is different from Rayner's celebration of English pragmatism and empiricism, and, apart from Freud, the theorists most consistently mentioned are Ferenczi and Laplanche—analysts intensely concerned with the implications of adult sexuality for the sexuality of the child, committed to the further elaboration of the emphases of the early Freud, and, until recently, very often ignored by British clinicians.

André Green reads Winnicott historically through the British Psychoanalytical Society and the profound effect upon it of Melanie Klein and her reorganization of Freud. He sees this as part of the more general fate of the Freudian legacy and the challenge it posed to contemporary thought and society, then and now. In a lecture at the Squiggle Foundation in 1991 (Abram, 2000), Green had discussed the distinctions between psyche, soul, mind, and intellect in Winnicott's work, and he here returns to them to argue that Winnicott's emphasis on emotional development went beyond that common in the British Society, to take "the form of a sort of *incarnation*, the result of the dwelling of the psyche in the body, where the psyche is an intermediate structure between the organism and the environment". He proposes to extend the work on the transitional to intermediate structures *within the internal world* and, potentially, to the essential structure of the ego itself. And he insists that the location of the object outside omnipotent control, which is fundamental to the establishment of the self, cannot be accomplished without destructiveness.

Beginning from his own disagreements with Laplanche's criticism of Winnicott's idea of the first "not-me" possession, Dominique Scarfone is interested in drawing out the similarities between two writers he admires. In discussing the actual meaning of "the object" and of what is implied by "use" in "The Use of an Object" (1971h), he too insists on the place of destructiveness in the constitution of the self. At the stage of object-relating, the object is not an object because there is no differentiation and "an indistinctness" reigns "between the experience (emotion) and the object". Nonetheless, the infant in the unintegrated state is subjected to the impact of otherness through the care of the adult, and in Laplanche's account this implies a "generalized seduction" through which psychic sexuality is implanted in the child's psychological structure. Scarfone focuses on the time horizon involved in the existence of a self-reflexive "I" and the impossibility of introjection and projection from the start. He ascribes two different meanings to "projection" in Winnicott's paper, the one at the stage of object-relating to be understood to "imply that knowledge of the object amounts to the *emotional experience* implied in relating and that "one could argue that *the reality of the object is the emotional experience occurring within the subject–object compound*. That is, the experience embedded in the relating does not require the subject to be clearly differentiated from the object." The word "projection" at this stage is used in the sense of a *denial* of any sense of separateness. At a later stage, projection proper—aimed at abolishing separateness—is retrospectively introduced as a template for the earlier phenomenon. Laplanche's emphasis on seduction and its transformation into a general framework for structuring the psyche and the analytic situation are seen as supplementing and complementing Winnicott.

Andreas Giannakoulas traces the shifts in meanings and understandings of the primal scene within Freud's own development and then in later writers, attributing to Winnicott a new *"fertile* perspective" where "the instincts serve the self, they do not constitute it". In emphasizing the fundamental impact of the parents' own unconscious world, he, like Scarfone, as well as Mario Bertolini and Francesca Neri, links Winnicott with Ferenczi and Laplanche in the importance attributed to the parents' unconscious messages and the child's attempts to make sense of them. Giannakoulas quotes a passage from *The Piggle* which, he suggests, is the frankest statement of sex in accounts of child analysis. The importance of transgenerational transmission, the mother's pathology, and the impact of the parental unconscious for the possibilities open to the infant is raised here, as it is by most of the contributors. All of this argues for a Winnicott for whom sex and sexuality are fundamental.

Joyce McDougall's paper takes Freud's psychosexual stages and the creative potential of sublimatory activities to discuss the need to create, and the profound factors inhibiting creativity. She links a Winnicottian sense of the place of creativity in all human activity to sexuality, especially pregenital sexuality, and stresses the sexually infused dimensions of any creative endeavour. She, too, recuperates violence and aggression for the project of becoming human.

Helen Taylor Robinson reads Winnicott 's paper on transitional objects and transitional phenomena in parallel with a reading of John Donne's "The Good-Morrow". She argues that art enlarges the domain of what psychoanalysis can usefully discuss, and she uses this to establish a set of links between adult sexual exchange and its utilization of and development from infantile pleasures. An interest in the overlap between adult love and infantile regression is shared with Giannakoulas, and she too touches upon the availability in the unconscious of the earliest sensations and of the conditions within which they may be risked in adult sexual pleasure.

Mario Bertolini and Francesca Neri begin their paper with a moving reading of Rilke's poem, *Orpheus, Eurydice, Hermes* and the potential conflicts with which the Orpheus of the poem could have been torn. They use this to draw out a dimension of the poem which, for them, reflects Rilke's approach to "feeling real". In exploring this terrain they link Rilke with Winnicott in their case study of a late adolescent who initially comes to analysis because of his sense of not feeling real. Despite the existence of much clinical material concerned with his need for sex, feeling or not feeling real remains the major issue. Bertolini and Neri discuss this in terms of the adolescent's split between sex and sexuality and the processes required for them to be brought together.

In her account of two women patients referred to a national health clinic, Maggie Schaedel discusses how the origins of sexual dysfunction are to be found in failures within the early mother–child relation and an incapacity to play. In her exposition of these cases, Schaedel describes some of the difficult countertransferential issues that frequently arise in such clinical situations, and she describes her extensive use of Winnicott's work as a resource. Her chapter also demonstrates the connections between severe underlying pathology and its manifestation in sexual symptomatology.

In "Talking Nonsense, and Knowing When to Stop", first given as the Madeline Davis memorial lecture in 2003, Adam Phillips ranges across a series of interrelated issues to wonder about those situations where talking of ending does or does not make sense, and he insists on the impossibility of thinking endings and psychoanalysis together. This leads him to wonder about what does happen when an analysis stops, especially since the project of psychoanalysis incorporates the timelessness of the unconscious and the acknowledgement of loss. Phillips asks what may be implied in thinking about psychoanalysis as free association, and free association as the talking of nonsense. In his account, the person able to speak nonsense and be listened to is the person of interest to Winnicott, but speaking nonsense is harder to put together with desire. Phillips notes that Winnicott refers only rarely to free association, but play and the capacity to play are central. And yet the potentially different enterprises envisaged by Freud and by Winnicott under the rubric of psychoanalysis both recognize the disruptiveness of desire. Phillips puts Winnicott with Freud in the interrelation between sexuality and play, but Winnicott's own interest in play is predicated on play as possible only if the instincts do not cause too much disturbance to ego organization. This returns him to the place of sexuality in the consulting-room and what that recognition allows and restricts in the course of an analysis.

CHAPTER TWO

Winnicott
at the start of the third millennium

André Green

After the death of Winnicott, some psychoanalysts, as if waking from a nightmare lasting more than thirty years, began to ask if there were one psychoanalysis or many. Only now does an answer appear to have emerged, but one that seems to involve accepting so many models that one might wonder what the limits of an expansion that takes us so far from Freud's discoveries would be.

Without claiming any solution to this, it is clear that Freud's work, rooted as it was in his training and his culture, remained open-ended and ambiguous. It left aside a number of clinical and theoretical issues he either did not, or could not, deal with. Other psychoanalysts have continued his work in their own way, but this open-endedness has inevitably meant that developments have taken somewhat divergent directions. Psychoanalysis, however, cannot be a matter of taste or temperament.

In trying to analyse the work of Winnicott, I approach it from the perspective of some of the developments that took place in the British Psychoanalytical Society. This was just one possible direction within psychoanalysis, born of many others, but one that, despite conflicts and disagreements internal to this group, also shared a set of common traits that characterized the British Society. Developments that blossomed in France, Latin America, or the United States followed very different directions, even when no language barrier prevented the communication of ideas and concepts.

At the beginning of the 1980s, when I lamented to W. R. Bion the Babelian situation in psychoanalysis, he wisely replied that, before arriving at a universal language in psychoanalysis, one had—theoretically speaking, of course—to go to the extremes of one's particular idiom.

Today, psychoanalysis looks like a language spoken in many tongues. Most of the time, people, especially in multiregional or international meetings, pretend to understand each other, or even believe they do, to save losing face. But no actual discussion takes place, and even when there is no agreement at all, we fall into the trap of compliance (a Winnicottian notion) to keep the analytic body apparently united. This is a pretence of tolerance: behind the silence, there is frequently disagreement, disapproval, contempt, if not total misunderstanding.

To fully understand the relationship that I want to describe inevitably involves a return to Freud. Although it is impossible to do him justice, he is the starting point for all further developments, and I am mainly concerned with what has become of the Freudian legacy. I shall limit myself to a brief comment on the *Outline of Psychoanalysis* (Freud, 1940a [1938]), with the idea that in this last book—his last word on psychoanalysis—he restricts himself to the fundamentals.

The legacies of Freud and Winnicott

Like Winnicott's *Human Nature* (1988), an unfinished and nevertheless very useful resource, Freud's *Outline* is also unfinished. Nonetheless, it is a suitable platform from which to approach Winnicott's own agreements and disagreements with Freud. First, a reminder from Winnicott himself:

> Almost every aspect of whole relationships between whole persons was touched on by Freud himself, and in fact, it is very difficult now to contribute, except by fresh statement of what is

accepted. Freud did the unpleasant thing for us, pointing out the reality and force of the unconscious, getting to the past anguish and conflict which invariably lies at the root of symptom formations, and putting forward, arrogantly if necessary, the importance of instinct and the significance of childhood sexuality. Any theory that denies or bypasses these matters is unhelpful. [1988, p. 36]

A bon entendeur, salut!

But I want to underline the points on which they part. There are a number of limited but meaningful differences that are important, and I list them here because there is no possibility of an exhaustive examination.

1.   Freud defended the idea of a *psychic apparatus*. It is easy to understand why the image of an apparatus to define the psyche seems unpleasant and even shocking from a humanistic point of view, and Winnicott never uses this construct. Freud's view neglects the perspective of relationships, apart from those established within the apparatus. I would like to defend the idea of an apparatus from an abstract point of view—it is very difficult to defend it epistemologically, but, within Freud's theoretical organization, the concept of an apparatus enabled him to emphasize that the mind, like the brain, split into different phylogenetic formations, was not a unified structure but was divided into different "agencies" in conflict, in antagonistic and agonistic relationships. They belonged to different stages of evolution. The mind was, therefore, more heterogeneous than homogeneous—and the apparatus had the task of making these dissonant agencies work together in spite of their different regimen. This was even more important in the second topographical model because of the increased differences between the agencies of id–ego–superego, compared with the earlier view of conscious, preconscious, and unconscious processes. Consciousness, however, is their common nucleus. Moreover, there is this idea, specific to Freud, that the whole personality is based on a primitive terrain, the id, a great part of it inherited, with all further developments (ego, superego) the result of direct or indirect differentiations of this primitive nucleus. These markedly differentiated agencies all bear the hallmark of their origin: made in id.

2.   This raises the question of the *instincts*. Winnicott did not oppose the importance of the instincts or of the id. He even considered that a good integration of instincts was responsible for vitality and originality. But, for him, the instincts could have an influence on the development of the self, seen as a unity from the start, only after more urgent problems that are fundamental to mental health, such as integration, have been secured. For Freud, in the beginning everything is id, but for Winnicott, a minimal structure of the self must be built before the instincts can be recognized. This difference is still a matter of debate that takes different forms according to the approach favoured. Freud gives several reasons for the importance of the instincts or the drives:

a.   They are a structure at the limit of body and mind, which implies a measure of work for the mind—because of its connections with the body—to respond to its needs.

b.   They constitute a continuous permanent excitation, which can only stop with gratification.

c.   They are connected with the basic experience of pleasure–unpleasure, and they organize desire, wishes, fantasy.

d.   Most of the time, a drive needs an object for its satisfaction.

e.   The drive is experienced through its representatives; the instinctual is the representative of bodily excitation and is expressed mainly through object–thing and word representations. Both are combined in the concept of ideational representation.

Since all other concerns are secondary for Freud, the question becomes: "Are the drives linked with, or do they come into play after, more primary, and supposedly more urgent, tasks have been consolidated, and if so, what are these tasks?"

3.   For Freud, the necessity is for the individual to cope with the exigencies of *inner reality*, which is under the pressure of needs and drives; *outer reality* emerges only after the loss of the objects that once brought satisfaction (negation). For Winnicott, the object does not exist from the beginning—or, to put it more precisely, there is first a subjective object born from omnipotence, inseparable from the self, and, only secondarily, an objectively perceived object, once

the separation between mother and child has occurred. This conception is closer to Freud's thinking than to Melanie Klein's, but on the other hand Winnicott disagrees with them both about the death instinct.

4.   For Freud, *infantile sexuality* has the lasting role. It is the motor of development, the source of all significant changes. Winnicott recognizes that it must not be neglected, but he would not see it as the most important (because of his observations on borderline and psychotic patients). We see this clearly in the clinical material he uses to illustrate his ideas. For Winnicott, the overall importance of the Oedipus complex is present exclusively in neurotic patients, and he would assert that, in many cases, there is a total absence of signs indicating its presence. In this respect, Winnicott stands more with Klein than with Freud. Here, I think it is useful to distinguish between an oedipal structure, present in all human beings, however regressed they may be, and the appearance of the Oedipus complex, with different variations, positive, negative, with prominent pregenital traits, and so on, at a specific stage of infantile sexuality. It should be noted that the absence of oedipal features does not mean that an oedipal structure is not present: it can be repressed or split off or too weak to be of any help. This would be to confuse a manifest content and a latent one. Until now, to create a human being, we have to match elements belonging to two different sexes, and this also relates to a difference of generations. Consequences of clonage are unpredictable for the structure of the mind.

5.   This leads to the question of *bisexuality*. Though Winnicott's implicit criticism of Freud's account of bisexuality can be discussed, his own idea of a pure feminine element which has nothing to do with drives also requires thorough discussion, since there seems to be a confusion with narcissistic communication, which is different in essence from the drives. *If the pure feminine element is linked to being, "pure" means non-sexual. It would be better to label it in terms of non-objectal libido = ego libido = narcissism.*

6.   One unnoticed point of agreement between Freud and Winnicott concerns the *centrality of the dream*. The *Outline* puts the

interpretation of dreams at the core of the analytic discovery and the practice of analysis. There, Freud writes:

> But what makes dream so invaluable in giving insight is the circumstance that, when unconscious material makes its way into the ego, it brings its own mode of working along with it. ... It is only in this way that we learn the laws which govern the passage of events in the unconscious and the aspects in which they differ from the rules that are familiar to us in waking thought. [1940a (1938), p. 167]

This is a quotation with which any psychoanalyst would agree, but such an agreement stops short at the question of how we interpret dreams! Freud, Klein, and Winnicott are all in disagreement here.

7.   In Winnicott's *Therapeutic Consultations*, dreams are quoted twenty-eight times, more than any other item. For instance, he writes, about Case VII, Alfred (age 10 years): "One of the aims in this game (the Squiggle), is to reach the child's core and so to his fantasy and so to his dreams. A dream can be used in therapy since the fact that it *has been dreamed and remembered and reported* indicates that the material of the dream is within the capacity of the child, along with the excitements and anxieties that belong to it" (Winnicott, 1971f, p. 115).

8.   In "Dreaming, Fantasying, and Living" (1971a), a gem of a paper, Winnicott emphasizes the role of *formlessness* (a point on which he agrees with Bion), "which is what the material is like before it is patterned and cut and shaped and put together" (p. 33). In other words, dreams are forms. For Winnicott, formlessness applies to dream activity in general, as contrasted with dreaming (p. 35). It is obvious that this chapter is referring, critically, to the Kleinian technique of systematically interpreting fantasying activity. Implicitly, Winnicott's criticism is closer to *The Interpretations of Dreams* (Freud, 1900a). Winnicott is on the side of Freud against Klein. One could say that he has replaced fantasy by play, where the second is not understood as a surrogate of the first.

9.   The main differences between Freud and Winnicott are about *object relationships*. I wish to make a difference between the object as structure (subjective, or objectively perceived), which is not basically different in Freud and in Winnicott, and the object relation-

ship. Madeleine Davis (Davis & Wallbridge, 1981) has rightly emphasized that Winnicott could not be a paid-up member of the object-relations movement that originated with Fairbairn and Klein. But what should be stressed here is the way Winnicott understood that approach. For instance, he did not agree with the idea of the existence of an ego (a self) and of an object from the start; he believed in a non-integrated state to be distinguished from disintegration. We recall his remark about the importance of the interplay between two curtains, where it is the overlapping, without intrusion, and the separation, that is important, rather than Freud's distinction between inside and outside or Klein's concern with introjection and projection as the basic mechanisms of object relationships. Observable facts about an awareness of an object for the newborn do not prove that the object is seen as separate and distinct. It can still be a subjective object, which does not mean that it is internal.

In his paper "Metapsychological and Clinical Aspects of Regression within the Psycho-Analytical Setting" (1954a), Winnicott expresses a clear statement about Freud. In a detailed and direct comment, he says that Freud's work is explained by his choice of patients who had been *"adequately provided for in earliest infancy"*, the psychoneurotics (p. 284). He adds that Freud's own personal history was such that he came to the Oedipus complex or the prelatency period in his life as a whole human being ready to meet whole human beings and ready to deal in interpersonal relationships. He observes that Freud took for granted the early mothering situation, without being aware of the implications of it. Later, he postulated the pregenital phases of instinctual development but insisted that this work could not be complete because it was not based on the study of patients who needed to regress in the analytic situation.

To fully emphasize the material related to pregenitality, Winnicott perhaps neglects an important issue, a turning-point in Freud's work as far as theory and technique are concerned—that is, the analysis of the Wolf Man. It took time before psychoanalysts accepted the idea that Sergei Pankejeff was a borderline case. Melanie Klein was one of the first to correct Freud's interpretation, and even if one disagrees with her interpretation, she was aware of the inadequacy of Freud's account.

In developing his own ideas, Winnicott gives a very interesting account of Freud's clinical setting as compared to contemporary experience. He states clearly his own thesis on the role of environmental failure at a very early stage in psychotic illness. For him, the setting reproduces the early mothering techniques and invites regression, a regression as an attempt to return to early dependence. Progress has to be related to the true self—becoming able to meet environmental failure. Sometimes, a false analytic self may result from an "analysis", with the unconscious compliance of the analyst. Psychotic illness needs a specialized environmental presence interlocked with the patient's regression. The complex processes of individual growth can then be studied.

10.   The Freudian theory linking childhood experience and the building of the unconscious lies in his well-known model of *hallucinatory wish-fulfilment* as the basis for the formation of the primary processes, the construction of the wish as forming the settlement of the unconscious, the formation of the mnemic-traces that, reworked, give birth to desire, to the normal propensity of primary processes to take a hallucinatory route, and so on.

For Winnicott, this situation does not reflect a primary basic structure but happens only when the dwelling of the psyche in the soma and the body (notice Winnicott's differentiation between them) and a relationship to reality have been achieved. *This is a basic difference between Freud and Winnicott*, which probably relates to the fact that Winnicott was a paediatrician. At the beginning of his work, Freud was concerned with the difference between perception and representation. Hence his interest in the problem of hallucination and its function as linked to the unconscious. Winnicott was mainly concerned with the child's first anchoring in reality to ensure security.

Historical remarks on Winnicott and Klein

The time is coming when no further expansion of physical paediatrics will be needed and an increasing number of young paediatricians will be forced into child psychiatry. I long for the day, and have longed for it for three decades. But the danger is that the painful side of the new development will be avoided, and an attempt will be made to find a way around. Theories will be reformulated, implying that psychiatric disorder is a product not of emotional conflicts but of heredity, constitution, endocrine imbalance and crude mismanagement. But the fact is that life itself is difficult and psychology concerns itself with the inherent problems of individual development and of the socialization process; moreover, in childhood psychology, one must meet the struggles that we ourselves have been through, though for the most part we have forgotten these struggles or have never been conscious of them. [Winnicott, 1988, p. 10]

These observations are still valid today (just think of the importance given, say, to the transmission of the genes, the dysfunction of brain processes, disturbances of neurotransmitters, attachment theory).

Winnicott's initiation into psychoanalysis was accomplished under Melanie Klein's influence. Having talked to James Strachey, his analyst, about his ideas on manic defence, Strachey advised him to meet Klein. This was the start of a long and complicated relationship. She supervised some of his cases and recognized his obvious skills for child analysis, as she later proposed he treat her children, while also asking that he would go into supervision with her—an impossible situation, both psychoanalytically and ethically, and one of the multiple signs of the madness of the analysts at that time, Freud included, who is supposed to have analysed Anna. Winnicott, of course, refused. Later on, he had to face another difficult situation when his second wife, Clare, wishing to have an analysis, asked him if he would mind her going to Melanie. Another impossible situation, but one to which he, of course, did not object. It is often reported by those who knew him that, all his life, Winnicott hoped that Melanie Klein would eventually quote him and recognize his work significantly in her writings or lectures, but she died without doing so. I doubt she could understand what he meant, just as there is no evidence she understood her pupil, Wilfred Bion. On the other hand, as Alexander Newman (1995) has shown, there are more than a hundred citations of Klein by Winnicott. Unfortunately, since Newman's book has no entry on Freud, there is no specific information about him. Winnicott was President of the British Society when the *Standard Edition* was published, and his former analyst, James Strachey, had played a major role in the translation. In *The Language of Winnicott* (Abram, 1996), Freud is quoted thirty-eight times and Melanie Klein only twenty-five. Adam Phillips's book on Winnicott (1988) has forty-six entries for Freud and fifteen for Melanie Klein; Eric Rayner's book, *The Independent Mind in British Psychoanalysis* (1991), of which Winnicott was a major representative, mentions Freud on twenty-five occasions, Klein and the Kleinians nineteen. These figures may be understood as showing a kind of consensus that, despite the strong attraction to Kleinian ideas, Winnicott's main reference was—and, for the other Independents, still is—Freud.

Nonetheless, a distinction must be made between Klein and the Kleinians. Such is the case for Bion. Winnicott addressed five letters to Bion and mentioned him several times in his correspondence with others, though there is no trace of any answer by Bion. On 7 October 1955, Winnicott wrote: "I would like to say that I think of you as the big man of the future in the British Psychoanalytical Society" (Winnicott, 1987, p. 89). Winnicott regretted that some speakers were building a wall between Bion and the British Society, as if to protect him from the other members by creating some sort of insulation. In the same letter, he spoke of Melanie Klein as a "lovable person to whom I owe as much as I do to Freud", but he objected that "her followers stood together as a block and that there is no entry into this block except by the process of being analysed by Mrs Klein or by someone analysed by her, and so on" (p. 90).

It is of the greatest interest to read Winnicott's alternative interpretations of the material presented by Bion on the occasion that preceded this correspondence. He ends his letter to Bion: "I think we have very exciting times in front of us on the scientific ground in psychoanalysis. I hope the political scene will not go on spoiling the scientific work" (p. 95). Wishful thinking . . .

In *The Spontaneous Gesture* (1987), there are letters addressed to some of Melanie Klein's followers, disapproving of their attitude towards her: they were behaving like supporters instead of really discussing her views. Too much approval could not help "Mrs Klein" to improve her thinking. Much earlier, Winnicott had disapproved of the solution to the Controversial Discussions, which had accepted a kind of inner splitting between fractions of the British Society. He implored both leaders and their supporters to give up their disagreements and to reject the formation of separate groups. He also disapproved of Glover's resignation from the British Society.

While appreciating Winnicott's efforts to prevent the consequences of splitting between the groups and his attempts at reconciliation, there also appears to be an attempt at an avoidance of conflict, even when positions were irreconcilable. In a letter to J. O. Wisdom (26 October 1964), Winnicott complains about "the terrific opposition of Melanie" (p. 145) and continues: "Bion goes deeper than Melanie . . . or finds a way of stating what Melanie would not allow." But he also thought that what Bion was trying to say, he, Winnicott, had been trying to defend for two and a half decades. This was also the case for disputes abroad. For example, in a letter to Jacques Lacan (11 February 1960), he regretted the split in Paris. He remained in contact with the French psychoanalysts W. Granoff, V. Smirnoff, and Maud Mannoni, and when the *Nouvelle Revue de Psychanalyse* was created by J.-B. Pontalis, Masud Khan was asked to be a member of the editorial board. Winnicott's work was already well known in France, but this extended his readership considerably, and many of his books were then translated. He was, at one time, more influential in France than in England!

Winnicott's criticism of Melanie Klein

Melanie Klein was a "*maître à penser*", unlike Winnicott. He would not agree to be a master. Here we see the difference between an organized Kleinian movement and the absence of a truly Winnicottian group: his ideas are scattered among individuals who are, sometimes, also critical of them. The absence of dogmatism is fortunate, but, unfortunately, it does not pay when confronted with militant block factions. In 1962, Winnicott was invited by the candidates of the Los Angeles Psychoanalytical Society to give his views on the Kleinian approach. When Glover had written his uncompromising criticism of Melanie Klein, "An Examination of the Klein System of Child Psychology (1945), it had not managed to convince as many people as the author wished, because of the obviously personal tone of his criticism. In a similar situation, Winnicott chose a more objective and neutral attitude, and his paper essentially has an autobiographical quality. He starts by mentioning the Anna Freud–Melanie Klein Controversies and explains that Anna Freud was less important than Melanie Klein, because, when Freud and his daughter arrived in England, Klein had already established herself and was well known. Consequently, Klein resented Jones encouraging and helping the Freuds to move to England and saw it as an act of betrayal towards her.

Relating his own experience to his beginnings, Winnicott describes how his background as a paediatrician had made him familiar with disturbed children under the age of 4 or 5 years, which, for him, meant before the oedipal stage. He thought of himself as a pioneer, since all the theory at the time was centred on psychoneurosis and the Oedipus complex. When Winnicott went to Melanie Klein for an informal supervision, he was very impressed by what she knew about children, and he understood the importance of the analytic work being done on the basis of anxieties related to pregenital drives. Winnicott reported a case where the material of the analysis of a girl was clearly oedipal, though her symptom (anorexia) had started the day of her first birthday. Klein told him that, for her, there was no difference between adult analysis and child analysis and that no variations of technique were needed with children. The interpretations, as with adults, were transference interpretations. Winnicott had reservations about Klein's theory of the paranoid–schizoid position but considered the depressive position her most important contribution. All these discoveries were made before World War II. Nevertheless, Winnicott also thought she was mistaken because she pathologized normality: "deeper in psychology does not always mean earlier" (1962, p. 177). According to him, good-enough mothering makes these positions unimportant until the ego organization enables the baby to use projective and introjective mechanisms in gaining control over objects. If there is not enough good mothering, instead of a paranoid–schizoid position chaos occurs. Winnicott objected to Klein's tendency to push the age at which mental mechanisms appear further and further back, a criticism shared by many of her opponents, and he disputed her conspicuous neglect of the environmental factor. Nonetheless, he concluded, "The only important thing is that psychoanalysis, firmly based on Freud, shall not miss Klein's contributions" (p. 178). This is a paper of great clarity, written in 1962 to be given to American candidates.

Elsewhere, Winnicott developed many other criticisms. Despite a second analysis with Joan Riviere, who tried to complete the work started with James Strachey, Winnicott was not convinced by Kleinianism. He particularly objected to the extensive and exclusive use of the concept of internal object, with no consideration for the environment. But his own aim was not to study the role of the external object as such but to consider how an activity of the mind, conveyed by the environment—especially, the mother's mood or, worse, her hidden pathology—influences and moulds the infant's psyche. Hence the frequent occurrence of false-self organizations is to comply with the mother and sacrifice the true self, which is closely related to the drives and regarded by Winnicott as a sign of vitality. Freud, on the other hand, would think of repression as a primitive mechanism that is independent of the mother's influence. It is not only that Winnicott denied Melanie Klein's basic mechanisms at the outset; he could not agree with their presence from the beginning, just as he opposed some of Freud's views on the origins of psychic life. For him, both Klein and Freud were wrong in their assumptions, because they were not interested in understanding the importance of mothering. Both wanted to emphasize the inner world exclusively, as if the part played by the object were negligible. To some extent, it could be said that if Anna Freud was mainly interested in the role of the external object, and Melanie Klein in the role of the internal object, Winnicott wanted to evaluate the contribution of the environment in the building of the psychic world and in the creation of a third category of objects, transitional objects, part of transitional phenomena and occurring in transitional space as potential space.

Winnicott also objected to the widespread use of projective identification. In a letter (Winnicott, 1987), he complains that the expression had recently been used a hundred times in the British Society, and he says the same about envy. In other words, Winnicott objects to the uncritical adoption of Melanie's ideas by the members of the Klein group. He puts himself in the position of the black sheep, stubbornly undisciplined. All of this raises the problem of what Bion calls basic assumptions.

Let me compare the legacies of Winnicott and Klein by comparing their last books, *Playing and Reality* (1971e) and *Envy and Gratitude* (1957), which I consider landmarks of the psychoanalysis of the second half of the twentieth century, in which their respective authors go uncompromisingly to the extremes of their thinking. Klein's book appeared three years before she died, and Winnicott's was published posthumously, so they really do represent their last thoughts.

In *Envy and Gratitude*, Melanie Klein develops at length her concept of envy, whose usefulness would later be questioned by Herbert Rosenfeld. There have been many studies on envy, especially a memorable one by Walter Joffe (1969), but in her book Klein describes the greedy and destructive introjection, of which envy is the corresponding projection, as opposed to the generosity of gratitude. On reading the book, it is difficult not to see gratitude as bound to the patient's submissive attitude to the analyst's interpretations, and the acceptance of them as proving an absence of envy towards the supposedly nurturing breast. But even this has been questioned, by Betty Joseph, who regards too much approval as suspect. This leads to a total impasse. If the patient disagrees, he is overtly destructive; if he agrees, he is suspected of hiding his destructive envy. One gets the impression that a Kleinian analysand must fit exactly the picture the Kleinian analyst has of him. Isn't there a danger of a false self by submission to the analyst's beliefs?

This book contains a strong emphasis on the death instinct, expressed in a way that differs from Freud. In order to fight against the threat of annihilation, the child uses excessive projective identification. The child experiences oral gratification with excessive envy, which acts as a stimulus towards the intensification of genital desires and trends. Once more, genitality is seen primarily as a defensive flight from orality, rather than as the final aim of infantile sexuality. For Klein, the aim always regresses to the primitive one; puritanism is back. The primal scene is now labelled the "combined parent figure". Pleasure in sexuality and genitality is lost en route because priority is given to the good breast, frequently said to be an idealized one, and if penis envy is mentioned, it has to be re-interpreted as a screen against an envy of the breast. This is a long way from Freud. The good breast is a synonym of creativity of a very localized and unique sort. Throughout the book, the dominance of the oral relationship overshadows all the other hypotheses of psychoanalytic theory. The Other is no more than the breast.

It is obvious that Klein had the feeling of having discovered something very important with envy, and that, in some way, she tried to reformulate both her own theory and the entire theory of psychoanalysis through this new perspective. If envy is added to the "combined parent figure", we arrive at a point where sexuality is entirely absorbed by destructiveness. This leads to a technique of intensive, so-called deep interpretations, given as many times as the analyst feels necessary, and at the risk of force-feeding the patient. The implication of these views for the interpretation and handling of transference is openly different from the conclusions of the majority of psychoanalysts. I am struck by the fact that we psychoanalysts unconsciously come back to this technique, to a subtle form of suggestion.

Finally, let us observe that the book includes one mention—in a footnote—of Winnicott, about his concept of the "illusory breast". This would be ridiculous were it not tragic!

Playing and Reality, published fourteen years later, registers a considerable difference from *Envy and Gratitude*. Not only does the book contain new ideas for psychoanalytic theory, it also shows a burst of creativity on Winnicott's part, probably encouraged by the premonition of the proximity of his death. It is interesting to have a look at the list of references. Beyond the familiar psychoanalysts present in most books, there are the names of Bruno Bettelheim, Michel Foucault, L. C. Knights, Jacques Lacan, Arthur Miller, Charles Schultz (the author of Peanuts), William Shakespeare, Lionel Trilling. This is a point in common with Bion, who considered the great geniuses of civilization—such as Bach, Beethoven, Rembrandt, Monet, for instance—as psychoanalysts. It would be of remarkable interest to compare the work of Winnicott and Bion, considering them as authors deriving their thoughts from Melanie Klein but reaching different conclusions.

Playing and Reality is so rich a book that it is impossible to summarize. I have shown elsewhere (in Kohon, 1999) how, in the re-writing of the paper on transitional objects and transitional phenomena in 1969, there is an intuition of the negative, a concept that, apart from the late Cecily de Monchaux long ago, only Winnicott and Bion (apart from my own work) mentioned. In the case material added to the final version of the paper on transitional phenomena, Winnicott says about the patient that, "she was only interested in the negative side of relationships" (1971g). He adds that what she was conveying to him about her resentment of her preceding analyst was that "the negative of him is more real than the positive of you" (p. 23).

I have already quoted Winnicott's comparison between dreaming and fantasizing, showing how the second could be used as a defence. He also shows how fantasying is linked to other futile activities: "All they did was to fill the gap, and this gap was an essential state of doing nothing while she [the patient] was doing everything" (1971a, pp. 29–30). Obviously, these observations of fantasies include a criticism of Klein and her followers about their understanding of the material and the technique used to analyse them.

But the essential interest of the book is that it enables Winnicott to develop his ideas on playing. In one very moving observation while Winnicott is having a conversation with a mother, he observes her child's behaviour and notices that the play of this child relates to the conversation he is having with the mother, giving it another expression. This is quite different from Klein's use of play, where the play is not taken into consideration in itself, but reduced to the fantasy that can be guessed behind it. Here, the play is considered in its own right and understood in its functional use. Playing and creativity are obviously connected. Winnicott shows how the creation stands between the observer and the artist's creativity. It is on this occasion that he develops the idea of a pure female element at play in a basic form of creativity, and related to the experience of being.

Playing and Reality also contains one of Winnicott's most important papers, "The Use of an Object and Relating through Identifications" (1971h), in which the need to let the patient experience the maximum of destructiveness is seen as necessary for the subject to place the object (analyst) outside his omnipotent control. The experience of destructiveness, a destructiveness that has nothing to do with aggression, is necessary for the fostering of the separation process. Or again, the mirror-role of mother's look is the only example I know from that time of a foreign psychoanalyst having the courage to respond to Jacques Lacan by proposing a critical and convincing view of his *stade du miroir*, a view, that, while recognizing its importance, also re-interprets it in entirely new terms and deepens its meaning. Klein's work has been widely and, for the most part, uncritically diffused, as, after some delay, was Lacan's. Both propagated with the same gospel-like quality; they are two opposing theories with which I disagree.

Critique of Winnicott

I consider Winnicott's work to be a contribution of great value to psychoanalytic theory, the most important contribution of the post-Freudian era, but this presentation would be incomplete if I were not to express some reservations about his technique. Here Linda Hopkins's valuable research (1998, 2000) on Masud Khan and her belief that Winnicott's wish to avoid conflict also influenced his psychoanalytic technique is important. While Winnicott cannot be blamed for Khan's malpractice or his disregard for the ethical rules of analysis, his responsibility goes well beyond referring patients to Khan, since, in trusting him, Winnicott indirectly caused considerable damage to these patients. Given how much he would have known about Khan from his analysis of him, I do wonder how Winnicott could have been so fascinated by him.

We are aware of certain aspects of his technique, not only through Masud Khan, but also from Margaret Little (1985, 1987) and Harry Guntrip's (1975) accounts of their analyses with him, and my main criticism of him is his belief that he should try unconditionally to cure his patients by representing—and to some extent creating—the image of a good-enough mother. It is my belief that Winnicott could not tolerate the situation where he would have to show the patient how destructive he himself was, despite the fact that, as we have seen above, he systematically interpreted the positive function of destructiveness. I believe he was wrong, as were many others before him—Reich, Rank, Ferenczi, Klein, Hartmann, Lacan. This is why we are still searching for the right technique and why it is not a question of blame. It started with Freud and has continued up to the contemporary intersubjectivists.

About Winnicott, I just want to emphasize that the analyst should not comply, by his passive attitude, with the destructiveness of the patient, and that he must firmly keep a clear mind and confront the situation without giving up neutrality, not so much to defend himself against the patient's destructiveness as to strongly underline the patient's need to face his own narcissistic destructiveness and, ultimately, the destruction of his own psychic processes through a mixture of paranoia and omnipotence. Here I reach a point of disagreement with Winnicott: ruthless love is not enough to explain destruction. The rage to destroy enjoyment by domination of others, and the annihilation of the other's individuality, may be considered as forms of omnipotence enhanced by an impotence produced by the patient's own narcissistic closure. Trends of this kind are not a form of love, even in its ruthless form: they are a culture of death. We are here beyond ambivalence and beyond any kind of love. We are facing destructive, disintegrative forms of negative narcissism to deny the existence of the other. This is a point that both needs further study and requires acknowledgement now.

From the beginning—Freud included—problems of technique that essentially relate to their curative power have always worried psychoanalysts. Someone, periodically, may claim to have the right answer, but it would be truer to say that we are still in search of it.

Conclusion

The essentials of Winnicott may be found in *Human Nature* (1988), a book he never succeeded in finishing but which can still be treasured for its very inspiring richness. I shall first quote the "Introduction to Part IV":

> Somewhat artificially I shall choose three different languages for the description of the earlier phenomena of emotional development. First I shall discuss

A. The establishment of a relationship with external reality, then

B. The integration of the unit self from an unintegrated state, and

C. The lodgement of the psyche in the body.

I can find no clear sequence in development that can be used to determine the order of description. [1988, p. 99]

In "The Posthumous Winnicott", a lecture given in 1991 at the Squiggle Foundation, I emphasized the distinctions between psyche, soul, mind, and intellect, which can only be found in Winnicott's work. The emphasis on emotional development is common to all the psychoanalysts of the British Society, but in Winnicott it takes the form of a sort of *incarnation*, the result of the dwelling of the psyche in the body, where the psyche is an intermediate structure between the organism and the environment. The self, according to Winnicott, is the result of a gathering together. Not only does it accomplish a unity of the person, it constitutes an "act of hostility to the not-Me" (1988, p. 124). Considering the body–mind problem, Winnicott proposes the idea that psyche is the *imaginative elaboration of body functioning*. Brain and intellect belong to characteristically different domains: "there is no meaning to the term intellectual health" (p. 12). "At first, there is soma, then psyche that in health gradually became anchored to the soma; sooner or later, a third phenomenon appears which is called instinct or mind (p. 12).

I strongly emphasize this position of instinct or mind as "*third*", standing between soma and psyche, and in my Squiggle lectures I developed my own ideas of thirdness and their challenge to the so-called two-body psychology. For me, there is always a three-body relationship (as in language: I, You, He/She), just as mother, father, and child constitute a basic triangle from the start. Winnicott observed that the words "I am" are the most dangerous ones in the languages of the world. The object is a separate entity. The object needs to be located outside the area of omnipotent control. This operation cannot be accomplished without some violence, a kind of mutation that cannot happen gradually, step by step. That is why destructiveness is unavoidable to ensure a separate identity.

The imaginative elaboration of the psyche leads to the creation of transitional phenomena, something known by mothers and caregivers from time immemorial but to which, before Winnicott, nobody paid much attention, as it seemed so natural. I consider it as fundamental to psychoanalysis; I also consider the area of illusion that is postulated by this description as enlightening and enriching Freud's thinking.

Finally I want to come back to Winnicott's provocative assertion that there is no meaning to the term "intellectual health" (1988, p. 12), as the boundaries between intellectual health and intellectual distortions of truth raise many problems. Of course, the boundaries between intellect, psyche, and mind are not easy to draw, though Bion's work can be helpful because his alpha-function has intellectual consequences for the search for truth. Even in illusion, there is a part played by the intellect, and I further believe that the characteristics of the transitional object have implications for the intellect, as do the acceptance of negative capability and Winnicott's well-known paradox between subjectivity and objectivity.

Winnicott dares to put forward an idea that also frightens him—that is, that in early development there is an intermediate state between primary narcissism, which he understands as the individual merging with the environment, and interpersonal relationships. He adds: "Between the mother, who is physically holding the baby, and the baby, there is a layer that we have to acknowledge which is an aspect of herself, and at the same time an aspect of the baby. It is mad to hold this view and yet the view must be maintained" (1988, p. 157). It reaches the limits of what is conceivable.

Here, I now wish to extend what Winnicott asserts. I believe that the concept of the transitional is not only valid between the inside and the outside, the object being, and not being, the breast, the *concept of the transitional* applies also to intermediate structures *within the internal world*. Though these processes take place internally, different parts, which all play a part in the internal, are in some cases also external to each other (for instance, the ego from the id, or the superego from the ego). This seems to imply passages from one place to another within the inner world. I propose that in these areas of movement, different logics are at play (for instance, the logic of the id and the logic of the ego), and create a third, on the analogy with symbolism, where we have the reunion of two separate fragments creating a third object formed by the reunification of the disjointed parts. This could apply equally both to the preconscious processes and to what I have called the tertiary processes. But I would go further and propose that the essential structure of the ego itself is of a transitional nature. This is consistent with Bion's idea, borrowing from Keats, of negative capability.

To celebrate the work of the authors we admire can sometimes include the extension, well beyond their formulations, of a concept they have introduced into our theory and which continues to be elaborated in our minds. To help us recreate our conception of the mind, we have to use the work of our ancestors—Freud, Klein, and Winnicott—each of whom built their ideas on the basis of different kinds of patients. Today, psychoanalytic experience has to rely on the greater frequency of non-neurotic structures. The more enlarged the basis for our description, the more accurate we are likely to be, because we have to go beyond neurosis which was Freud's reference point. The more complex our body of knowledge, the closer to truth our hypothetical views will be.

CHAPTER THREE

Laplanche and Winnicott meet . . . and survive

Dominique Scarfone

P sychoanalysis is a discipline in which debate is too easily avoided and where little cross-fertilization between different theoretical currents is allowed. This is regrettable, since psychoanalysis is thereby subjected to both dogmatic vagrancy from within and harsh epistemological criticism from without. In this chapter, I aim to show that fruitful confrontation is possible, at least when it is a matter of bringing together the views of authors who were able to develop an open-ended yet coherent set of concepts to account for the whole field of psychoanalytic practice.

Donald Winnicott and Jean Laplanche are two such authors. Their writings, at any given phase of their theoretical development, are grounded in a general set of principles and in concepts that are highly consistent, strongly interrelated, and firmly rooted in the Freudian framework.

The idea of making them "meet" emerged from a personal reluctance to leave out the one when consulting the other, despite their different (some would say divergent) perspectives. Both have been, and still are, powerful guides for my understanding of what psychoanalysis is about and for taking the original Freudian discovery fully into account while remaining open to refinements, new developments, and eventual revisions. I have long had the feeling that the discrepancy between these two authors is mainly a matter of a different vocabulary, itself reflecting a different psychoanalytic trajectory, and that they are in fact highly compatible. Here, I aim to illustrate how each of them "survives" a confrontation with the other, and how both theories may profit from the encounter. Ironically, my curiosity about their possible compatibility was triggered by Laplanche's rather marginal criticism of one of Winnicott's well-known expressions: that the transitional object is "the first *not-me* possession". According to Laplanche, it should be rather called "the first *me*-possession". In Laplanche's view, indeed, to call the transitional object a "first not-me possession" implies that there were only "me-possessions" prior to it, whereas he dismisses any "me" or "I" being there from the beginning. But my understanding has always been that Winnicott was just as doubtful of the presence of a "me" or "I" at the beginning of life. I therefore felt compelled to go deeper into the matter to see if the disagreement was real or just a misunderstanding.

A thorough discussion of this seemingly trivial question involves the examination of the whole *opus* of both authors, something well beyond the scope of this chapter, although I will be examining a broader arena than the initial "trigger". My aim is to show that, provided we do the work of exegesis required by the difference in their respective vocabulary and conceptual background, Laplanche and Winnicott are actually in agreement.

For this experiment, I have chosen one of Winnicott's most original contributions, generally considered representative of his thinking, "The Use of an Object and Relating through Identifications" (1971h)—hereafter referred to as "UO". I will "cross-examine" it through the concomitant use of a few of Laplanche's concepts that are, in turn, highly representative of his thinking. These are the notions of the "Copernican"—as opposed to the "Ptolemaic"—view of the subject in psychoanalysis, and that of "translation", as they were expounded in the context of Laplanche's "theory of generalized seduction" (Laplanche, 1989, 1997).

Setting the stage

There is always some violence done in summarizing a paper of such magnitude as "The Use of an Object", but in this case we are fortunate in having Winnicott's own summary identifying the various phases of theoretical development occurring throughout the text. At the end of his paper, Winnicott recapitulates those steps as: "(1) Subject *relates* to object. (2) Object is in process of being found instead of placed by the subject in the world. (3) Subject *destroys* object. (4) Object survives destruction. (5) Subject can *use* object" (UO, p. 94).

Laplanche's thinking is also much richer than the schematic picture conveyed by a brief presentation of a few key concepts. One of his main contributions to psychoanalytic thinking is the recovery of the seduction theory long after its abandonment by Freud, and its transformation into a general framework for the structuring of both the psyche and the analytic situation. The original Freudian theory invoked a perverse seduction of a child by an abusing adult. Freud replaced it, on the one hand, by the theory of inborn, unconscious primal fantasies and of endogenous infantile sexuality, and, on the other, with a softer version of the role of the adult, whereby the mother is the innocent seductress who can elicit erotic sensations in the child through ordinary care.

Laplanche considers that something fundamental was lost in this theoretical shift—namely, that regardless of anecdotal excitatory events, the child is born into a world replete with adult sexual messages that unconsciously contaminate every form of adult–child interaction. A trivial example is the mother breastfeeding her infant: she is obviously *feeding* the child, but she is also making use of her breasts, of highly invested *sexual* organs. She need not be aware of the erotic dimension of her motherly endeavour, yet something of her sexual being will unconsciously affect the child. This is an example of Laplanche's concept of the *enigmatic* or *compromised message* from mother to child: a message compromised by the adult's unconscious sexuality.

For Laplanche, "generalized seduction" is thus a universal process through which psychic sexuality is *implanted* in the child's psychological structure long before biological sexual maturation (puberty) is attained. He calls this "the fundamental anthropological situation". The time lag between reception of sexual messages and actual sexual maturity accounts for the irremediably enigmatic dimension of sexuality for children. The child is thus confronted with the task of constructing his own sexual theories and meanings, inasmuch as his intellectual and bodily development allow. In Laplanche's view, infantile sexual theories originate not from inherited primal fantasies, but from the endogenous work of translation whose primary result is twofold: part of the translation is integrated as an ego-syntonic content (in fact, it is part of the actual building of "ego"), while untranslatable residues constitute a permanent source of "irritation" or "provocation", eliciting still further efforts at translation. Throughout development, every new situation, endowed with its own enigmas, resonates with the untranslatable residues left behind by previous attempts at making sense of the adult's messages. These residues are grounded in the child's unconscious—they are its actual nuclei—and constitute the "source-objects" of the drives.

At this primal stage, then, "translation" equates with primary repression. Laplanche is actually making use of the translational concept of repression that Freud outlined in his letter to Fliess of 6 December 1896. Following this model, new translations and/or transcriptions of psychic content are made at subsequent phases of development, and repression is precisely the abandonment of previous translations in favour of newer forms. When, due to significant change in the existential framework, an existing version needs to be reconsidered, what cannot be converted into the new idiom is said to be repressed. To quote Freud: "A failure of translation—this is what is known clinically as 'repression'" (Freud, 1985, p. 208). Every new translation is therefore a way of repressing a former, obsolete one.

The translational model of the psychic work occurring in response to the enigmatic message of the adult accounts for the differentiation of the psychic agencies. This is where Laplanche's description of a Ptolemaic (ego-centred, like the Earth-centred universe of Ptolemy) versus a Copernican stance (where the centre lies outside of the ego) comes in. At first, there is no ground for attributing to the subject a sense of being at the centre of its universe. From the very beginning the infant is subjected to the impact of otherness. The gravitational centre of the system is not within the child; it is in the external significant adult and that adult's enigmatic messages[1]. However, through the sequence of *implantation* (of enigmatic messages), *translation* (though never fully achieved), and *differentiation* (of psychic agencies), a subjective closure is eventually attained, giving the subject the illusion of a universe that Laplanche would characterize as Ptolemaic, where the ego feels it occupies the central position. Otherness has not been abolished, however. The other is now internal and repressed, working as a foreign, though internal, body, an *it* or an *id*. Individuals normally adopt a spontaneous Ptolemaic stance, whereas the task of psychoanalysis is to reintroduce the Copernican view if it is to account for the significance of the unconscious in human existence.

It must be underscored that the Copernican stance, which, according to Laplanche, is essential to psychoanalytic practice and theory, is not simply a description of psychic reality from the third-person perspective, although it is compatible with such an account. Laplanche has in mind a more radical decentring than that conceived of by Copernicus with the heliocentric system of the planets; "Copernican" is therefore, in a way, a misnomer. The idea of a subject de-centred by the inherent otherness of the unconscious cannot be domesticated by simply locating a centre elsewhere: one must, rather, conceive of an intractable otherness, always there to disturb any attempt at positing "ego" as the source of the fundamental psychic events, even when it is someone else's "ego". In practice, it is a question, for instance, of whether or not the psychoanalytic conception of unconscious mechanisms is compatible with other plausible models of the mind (e.g., that of developmental psychology). In this regard, the notion of *projection* is one example where a strictly Ptolemaic view posits a working of the infant's mind that is not sustainable. Such an ego-centred conception clashes with the maturational neurological and psychological state of the infant, but it also clashes with the radical otherness implied by the Freudian concept of the unconscious as it emerges from Laplanche's close examination of Freud's theory. In this respect, Freud's own theory of innate primal fantasies can also be ascribed to a Ptolemaic, hence imaginary, stance. The feeling that these fantasies come strictly from within, or from a prehistoric past, is acceptable as a subjective impression on the part of the analysand;

but to elevate this to the status of a psychoanalytic theory of their actual origin is incompatible with contemporary scientific conceptions of evolution and of genetic transmission as much as it implies ignoring the ostensible impact of the other within the "fundamental anthropological situation" defined by Laplanche.

In this very summary account of some central ideas of Laplanche, I have stressed those that may seem to clash with some Winnicottian notions found in "The Use of an Object . . ." Think, for instance, of Winnicott's reference to projection, or the finding of the object. Aren't these what Laplanche would call "Ptolemaic" views? If so, aren't the views of Laplanche and Winnicott fatally opposing one another? To answer these questions, I shall now examine Winnicott's paper in detail, guided in this by his own summary.

1. "Subject relates to object"

In "The Use of an Object", *object-relating* is contrasted with *using an object*. Usage requires that the object be real and "not a bundle of projections". Indeed, at the phase of object-relating—not to be confused with true object relationship[2]—"projection mechanisms and identifications have been operating" (UO, p. 98).

At first, from a Laplanchian vantage point, this assertion looks problematic. Laplanche insists on establishing whether it is legitimate to ascribe projection to the infant's "ego". The question arises whether it is congruent with the actual status of the subject to infer that it is experiencing itself as a central (Ptolemaic) agency, by contrast actually to being in a decentred (Copernican) position. In the case of projection, especially considering such early stages of psychic differentiation, Laplanche considers a first-person stance, as in projection, highly questionable (Laplanche, 1990). I will try to show however, that, despite appearances, Winnicott's position and that of Laplanche do converge.

For this we must acknowledge that, at the stage of object-relating, the object is not actually known as an object. This is implicit since Winnicott's subsequent phase is described as "object in the process of being found". On the other hand, Winnicott asserts that at the stage of object-relating, "projection mechanisms and identification have been operating", thereby evoking Melanie

Klein's primitive introjection–projection cycle. A complex system is thus already in place that probably also carries a measure of consciousness. There is no reason, indeed, to deny the newborn baby some form of consciousness, if not yet a sense of being separate. The newborn's surrounding world is value-laden, at least in the sense that the experience it provides may be emotionally felt as either pleasant or unpleasant.

But the meaning of *projection* at this stage must be further qualified. If relating to an object, by contrast with using an object, rests on projection, and if the object has yet to be found, then the subject does not actually *know* that it is *relating*. While, from an external point of view, relating at any time can be described in terms of *subject* distinct from *object*, we are not able to assert, at the phase examined here, that the subject is *self-consciously* present as a fully distinct agent. This is a crucial aspect of the situation described by Winnicott, as is clear near the end of his paper when he notes that as usage becomes a fact, *projection* takes on a different meaning:

> As I see it, we are familiar with the change whereby projection mechanisms enable the subject to take cognizance of the object. This is not the same as claiming that the object exists for the subject because of the operation of the subject's projection mechanisms. At first the observer uses words that seem to apply to both ideas at one and the same time, but under scrutiny we see that the two ideas are by no means identical. *It is exactly here that we direct our study.* [UO, pp. 91, emphasis added]

We notice that Winnicott does not underline the apparent paradox of an early version of projection that entails no separation between subject and object. We must therefore presume that he deems the word "projection" valid in both the instances described in the cited paragraph, even if "the two ideas are by no means identical". How, then, are we to think of projection at the specific stage of object-relating? In what sense are the two ideas of projection not identical? In his customary parsimonious style, Winnicott does not clearly address all the aspects of the problem, but it can be argued that, at this stage, projection implies that knowledge of the object amounts to the *emotional experience* implied in relating.

Winnicott indeed writes that, at the phase of object-relating, projection *is the reason* the object exists. Hence, there is no question of
separateness; therefore one could argue that *the reality of the object is
the emotional experience occurring within the subject–object compound.*
That is, the experience embedded in the relating does not require
the subject to be clearly differentiated from the object. The word
"projection" at this stage is therefore a word used as a *primordial
denial* of any sense of separateness. The term, in this context, can
only be justified retrospectively, from the vantage point of a later
stage, when projection proper, aiming at regressively abolishing
separateness, provides the template for the earlier phenomenon.

   In dealing with this complex issue, Winnicott adopts a deeply
Freudian way of theorizing: it is redolent of how Freud introduced
primary identification retrospectively, as something theoretically
necessary for justifying secondary identification (Freud, 1923b). By
analogy, we feel justified in asserting that, in the first part of his
paper, Winnicott is really describing a *primary projection,* something quite different from, although not unrelated to, projection
proper. And if we concede that there is no difference between the
"subject–object compound" and the pleasant or unpleasant emotional experience, then *relating* really means "being in a given
emotional state". The subject exists, one could say, but it does not
yet know. The object also exists, but is not yet known. Differentiation will make its way in the next phase.

   At this stage of Winnicott's progression towards the theory of
the use of an object, what is important is the indistinctness between
the experience (emotion) and the object. Only in this way, and
probably not in terms of internal representation, can the object be
said to be subjective. On a purely cognitive level, there is no reason
to deny the baby mental representations, but this does not equate
with the sense of internality and externality that emerge at a later
phase. This is stated in "Fear of Breakdown" (Winnicott, 1963b)
where it is quite clear that at the early stages of development there
is no "I" to actually experience subjectively the breakdown that is
happening. The "I" stage is consecutive to that of object-relating, as
we shall see below. *Projection,* therefore, cannot at this stage be
thought of, even unconsciously, in the form of "I expel something".
It is really an experience where, looking back on it theoretically,
one can only detect the intention[3] to stop experiencing some un-

pleasant emotional state and to recreate the blissful non-separate-ness. Conversely, identification can be subsumed with introjection under the intention of keeping a pleasurable experience going on. "To put inside" (introject), at this juncture, means: "Let the good experience go on."[4]

In a strict sense, the space-oriented terms "projection" and "introjection" are inappropriate for describing psychic events at this stage, as spatial metaphors imply a sense of separation of subject from object, and this has not yet been attained. Until sepa-rateness is recognized, one can surmise that there is no mental *space*, since the mental-space metaphor demands a complex new development involving transitional objects and phenomena. The birth of *transitional space* is indeed a marker of the simultaneous birth, separation, and linking of external and internal spaces (Winnicott, 1953, 1971g). Until that is accomplished, a time-ori-ented vocabulary seems preferable for object-relating, as it does not ask *where* the experience is happening—a question that cannot possibly be asked without a sense of separateness—it just considers if it is actually going on, or if it has ceased.

If the foregoing interpretation of the "object-relating" phase is correct, then Winnicott's description does meet Laplanche's requi-site for a Copernican view of the subject. We have seen that a Copernican subject is de-centred insofar as the object, the other, comes before the subject. In object-relating, the emotional experi-ence takes place before there is an "I" there to record it as part of one's own "objective" history. This is conceivable in both Laplanche's and Winnicott's accounts.

Obviously, finding a convergence between the two authors does not require their descriptions to be identical. Instead, there is an interesting crossover between the two. As Winnicott directs his study at the difference between two meanings of projection in the progression towards the use of an object, in Laplanchian terms he is thereby demarcating a Copernican from a Ptolemaic form of pro-jection. The early, Copernican, form of projection entails the undif-ferentiated emotional experience as the main reality to be "known". Conversely, when Laplanche insists on the reality of the message that is *felt* yet *not understood*, and posits that it is "known" mainly as a quantity of excitement, he is implicitly referring to an emotional impact on the infant's psycho-soma. The two authors meet at this point where a rather unqualified affective experience is the reality at hand.

2. "Object is in the process of being found instead of placed by the subject in the world": the transitional and the translational

This second step in Winnicott's progression refers to the well-known Winnicottian paradox of the found-created object and its links with his theory of transitional phenomena and potential space. Finding the object supposes its presence in a world where it can be found. For Laplanche, such objective presence is also taken for granted. The object—the other, the adult—is the producer of the enigmatic messages that trigger the beginnings of psychic differentiation. In this part of Winnicott's paper, *process* is the important feature rather than clear-cut static pictures of phenomena.

"Object is in the *process* of being found" emphasizes that the finding of the object must be allowed to happen at its own pace. The illusion of omnipotence must be modulated through the elaboration of transitional space and brought towards new, more common forms of illusion such as are found in the cultural experience. If there is no demand that the found-created paradox be resolved, objects and phenomena may remain transitional and provide "a resting-place for the individual engaged in the perpetual human task of keeping inner and outer reality separate yet interrelated" (Winnicott, 1971g, p. 2).

Elaborating the intermediate space strongly correlates with the discovery of objective reality. "Object is in the process of being found instead of placed by the subject in the world": Winnicott's subtle yet precise language is here worth mentioning again. "To be placed in the world" is a sentence that can only be stated from the vantage point of the object, and I believe it is not mere chance that Winnicott used the passive form. This is consistent with the object's responsibility in attending a process where the child's subjective point of view is on its way but not yet there. It is a stage where both the psychic subject—that is, a subject endowed with, as it were, a *subjective* point of view—and its object are emerging together from the undifferentiated state that prevailed at the stage of object-relating. Thus, the external object, in order to be found, must allow the subject as much initiative as possible. In this sense, it can be said to be *passive*, even though it is certainly active in taking care of the child. If, however, the object's special and relative form of passivity is lacking, then impingement may ensue, with all its negative consequences.

Precisely the same remarks apply to Laplanche's *translational* model, and Winnicott's account may even refine the Laplanchian description to some extent. Translation, too, is a *process* during which the child's "I" has both to emerge as a subject (a centre of action) and be constituted into a coherent ego, whereas the residues left behind by the partial failure of translation constitute the repressed. For Laplanche, however, the subject is at first passive, insofar as it stands at the receptive end of the adult–child relationship as regards the enigmatic messages. Laplanche nevertheless acknowledges that the infant is *active* in other ways, particularly in its task of translating the adult's messages. The description of the Laplanchian object (*active* in emitting the messages and providing optimal care for the child) may gain in precision through Winnicott's idea of *passivity*. As we shall see below, faced with the process of translation occurring in the child's psyche, the adult object will need to tolerate remaining passive as the child makes its own moves towards discovery and construction of meaning.

What is striking is that both accounts identify a phase where the subject begins emerging with a sense of self, and therefore with a truly subjective stance—a Ptolemaic centre. This is another, more familiar, paradox: that one has to discover the object's objective existence to gain a true sense of subjectivity. Thus, in retrospect, it can be said that when Winnicott posits a subjective object before completion of the present task of finding it in the environment, the word "subjective" does not yet have the full meaning it will convey once a self-reflexive form of subjectivity has resulted from the finding. The dispute about "the first not-me possession" has then lost its *raison d'être*! "Me" and "not me" are not contradictory qualifiers of the transitional "possession": they come into existence simultaneously, through the same transitional (Winnicott) and translational (Laplanche) processes.

But the parallel does not stop there: Laplanche and Winnicott are on the same wavelength concerning objectivity and subjectivity in yet another way. Retrospectively, the object, in reality, has "been there all the time" (UO, p. 88) although for the infant it had no existence until it was found. The object was fully objective, but there was no subjective subject able to acknowledge this status. On the other hand, the subject was objectively present and acting, but without subjective awareness of its own doings.[5] Similarly, in the process of implantation and translation described by Laplanche, messages are objectively there, but they are only felt as *signals* that affect the infant while it cannot account for what is affecting it. The objective situation can be described in these terms only from the point of view of an observer, not from the baby's vantage point. Only when translation has reached a phase where the subject emerges—itself a result of translation—is it capable of conceiving of the signals as carrying some intentional meaning on the part of the object. At this later stage, although Laplanche does not mention any such thing, I would say that projection, following Winnicott's *later* meaning of the word, can take place and play its role in the cognizance of external reality.

A third sort of congruence between the two authors is also noticeable. Winnicott's second phase towards the use of an object, "Object in the process of being found", marks a transformation in the nature of the object itself. In the previous phase, Winnicott had mentioned that "relating to an object" implied an *alteration* in the subject (UO, p. 88). Here Laplanche helps us clarify Winnicott's idea. "Alteration" is indeed a term typical of the Laplanchian lexicon, since what "alters" the subject comes from the other (*alter*). One may then suggest that, in view of the reality of the message, and especially of its heterogeneous nature in regard to the infant's capacity, the subject–object complex is *altered from the beginning,* as from the start it carries the inherent *difference* between adult and child—namely, in terms of sexual maturity. Finding the object, following relating to it, is therefore a further differentiation happening within an already altered emotional complex. This is hardly surprising, since linguistically the very word *emotion,* with its meaning of being moved, unsettled, already implies a displacement of some sort from the resting state, so, literally, an alteration of that state. Hence, separation, which is also a form of destruction, has its roots in the heterogeneity *already present* in the subject–

object amalgam. The previously undifferentiated state contained the seeds of differentiation. A Ptolemaic subjective stance (the ordinary brand of illusion) is then called upon to mend a Copernican wound caused by the progression towards shared reality. A wound, that is, because as the object is discovered, so is dependence upon the object as well as the disproportionate enigma of the object's world.

3. "Subject destroys object": the meaning of destroying

Winnicott's subsequent phase, "Subject destroys object", is part of a process that "does not come about automatically, by maturational process alone" (UO, p. 88). Winnicott eventually invokes the infant's inborn aggressive drives but leaves unsaid why the baby would need to exert (even in fantasy) such destructive attacks on the object. I will try to describe my own understanding of what "destroying" means at this stage, but first I wish to highlight the idea that the inescapable *otherness* embedded in the subject–object relationship is probably an important source of what "destroying" there eventually is. A detailed description by Winnicott himself of what he means by destruction and the corresponding Laplanchian view are in order here.

For Winnicott "the object, if it is to be used, must necessarily be real in the sense of being part of shared reality, *not a bundle of projections*" (UO, p. 88, emphasis added). I have already examined how "projection" should be interpreted in this context. "Bundle" is now the word I wish to consider. As the etymology implies, a bundle is a group of things bound together. We have seen that, at the stage of object-relating, the projector was bound together with its projections, as these constituted the "object".[6] Now, for the object to cease being a "bundle of projections", the subject–object bundle is what must be unbound if there is to be an object in shared reality and if the subject is to find it and eventually "destroy" it in order to be able to use it. *But how is this achieved?*

Although destruction is the word I am using, this actual destruction belongs to the object's failure to survive. Without this failure, destruction remains potential. The word "destruction" is needed, not because of the baby's impulsion to destroy, but because of the object's liability not to survive, which also means to suffer change in quality, in attitude. [UO, p. 93]

Winnicott had previously mentioned that for the object "to survive" also means to "not retaliate" (UO, p. 91). Within this apparently simple description, there is a very complex picture where a series of mirror-like reflections between subject and object can create confusion in the reader. Let us forge ahead, step by step. In my reading of Winnicott, I suggest that destroying the object is tantamount to becoming an "I". This is presented elsewhere by Winnicott in the following terms: "I AM with the inherent implication I REPUDIATE EVERYTHING THAT IS NOT ME" (Winnicott, 1963b, p. 95). There is actually no better description of what a Ptolemaic closure may mean—a closure that is a cause for both triumph, as Winnicott's formulation suggests, and mourning, as we shall now see.

The baby destroys the object while coming to life as a subject, a self-reflective being, an "I". The "bundle of projections" contains the mirror reflections between self and object,[7] but we could hardly pinpoint the moment when a *self-reflective* process comes into being. It probably begins quite early, but one can only ascertain its existence when the perceptive–emotional complex of object-relating has been broken down into an I and an object in the shared reality—that is, when emotion and perception have become two separate things yet joined together by the transitional space. As mentioned earlier, the adult must let the infant spontaneously enter or leave a state where emotion and perception are bound together. That state is something that the infant can either wish would go on (introjection) or wish would cease (projection). Whereas in the previous, timeless framework, projection and introjection could be experienced as going on forever—that is, without any time-horizon—once a self-reflexive "I" has entered the scene the situation allows for a *perceived transition* between states. The progressive discovery of the object in the world introduces a time sequence: one state *follows* another, yet both subject and object remain essentially the same in their respective places. The experience of a sequence in *time* inaugurates the capacity for a metaphorical *space* in the mind. Thus, *time* and *space* now mark a dramatic new distance between subject and object and from now on will induce, respectively, the experience of the *passage of time* and the concurrent experience of *loss*. In this sense, the birth of the Ptolemaic experiencing of self is a cause for triumph as well as for mourning (Aulagnier, 1967).

The other consequence of the Ptolemaic closure is what Winnicott calls "destroying the object". We have already seen that what destruction there is actually resides in *the subject's own emergence*, in the differentiation taking place within the subject–object emotional complex described as "object-relating". The object is discovered and the discovery itself initiates the "destroying", in the sense that the object, from then on, will be located outside the realm of omnipotence. Why Winnicott should refer to this as "destroying" demands further clarification.

We saw Winnicott invoke the infant's inborn aggressive drive. On the other hand, he makes it clear that there is no actual destroying, that the real issue is for the object to survive by not retaliating. One may ask: what is there to retaliate or not retaliate to? And what kind of destruction is only potential? In this respect Laplanche's theory can shed some light. The enigmatic status of the adult's message rests on its being repressed. As we saw, in the translational model, repression actually means "a failure in translation". The adult's message therefore carries not so much semantic content as the impact, for the child, of some "quantity" that is mostly affect. But the infant's translation is a mainly inter-semiotic, by contrast with an inter-linguistic process, where the message must be *transformed* in such a way as to bring it, or part of it, to a state where it can be assimilated by the subject. Hence, translation entails not only the Ptolemaic closure of the subject, but also the subject's constant change, its perpetual "re-centring". The infant-translator is a producer of meaning, himself undergoing evolution, integration, and change in the process of emergence and differentiation that is the result of its own activity of translating. The construction of meaning implies a solipsistic condition, as even neuro-physiologists conclude from their experimental work on the brain (Freeman, 1999). Hence, the child builds its own internal references, those brought about by its inborn biological apparatus and by the responses that the external world elicits from its body–mind.

At this juncture, destroying steps in. Since the epistemophilic function of translation cannot be stopped,[8] when the child finds the object in the outside world—which is also outside the realm of its omnipotence—it can only feel an even stronger need to make sense of the object's existence, of its impact in terms of enigmatic messages and of the potential loss this represents. But for the child to construe a meaning concerning the object amounts to a form of destruction in that the solipsistic gulf created is a fundamental separation; the object must be ready to survive this by maintaining a link, lest it is really and tragically lost for the infant. I suggest that what *retaliation* means in this context can include every sort of impingement, but mainly *impingement upon the child's efforts to construct its own meanings.*

Obviously, a measure of impingement is inevitable since the child is brought up within a specific cultural group, that of the mother, amid a given set of cultural references that must be integrated lest the child remain a stranger in its own environment. This is what another French author, Piera Aulagnier, calls the mother's "primal violence" towards the infant, "the violence of interpretation" (Aulagnier, 1975). But such violence cannot be applied to everything that the child constructs without seriously damaging the child's own being. The primal and unavoidable "violence" is, in that case, substituted with "secondary violence", which in Aulagnier's terms indicates damage caused to the child's essential psychic functions, endangering its capacity to think. In Laplanchian terms, the normal process of "implantation of enigmatic signifiers" is replaced by "intromission", the violent and destructive variant of implantation where translation is hindered, as is the differentiation of psychic agencies. In this case, differentiation is felt by the child as a source of excessive pain or anguish, and retaliatory violence forces the child towards retreating into a state of submission, with its counterpart of imaginary omnipotence. Things can be even worse, pushing the child towards the undifferentiated state, where the subject–object emotional complex described earlier is reinstated and difference is not experienced any more. This is a condition, in short, where the object is once again just "a bundle of projections". If it persists, it can impede the discovery of the objective world. But if sufficient freedom is allowed for the child to construct its own interpretations, a benign form of illusion supersedes the omnipotent one. Here again, Winnicott's view that the "wish-fulfilling illusion may be the essential basis for all true objectivity" (Winnicott, 1951, p. 391) is fully compatible with Laplanche's conception of a Ptolemaic closure.

4. *"Object survives destruction"*

Winnicott and Laplanche also meet on the ground of the object's survival. For Winnicott *"there is no anger . . ."* in the destruction he refers to, "though there could be said to be joy at the object's survival" (UO, p. 93). To see what the object's survival may mean in terms of translation, let us turn our attention to what is implied in creating meaning—the solipsistic gulf that is thereby created. In terms of translation, survival of the object implies different things: first, that the message of the other is never completely processed, nor the other's presence ever abolished; second, that the object's being resilient not only means it is alive, it is also *interesting*.

The interest in the object does not rest solely on its reliability in satisfying the infant's basic needs. In Laplanche's theory, the object also carries a libidinal dimension whose very nature is seductive. There is, however, in this regard, at least one aspect of seduction in need of further elaboration. It is that the seductive nature of the adult–child interaction, granted it does not degenerate into perverse seduction, makes the adult all the more intriguing for the child, as a source of newer enigmas, ever-new motives for exerting the exciting function of translating and creating meaning.[9] It is as though the enigmatic message had triggered the epistemophilic drive in the child. The pleasure older children take in puzzles and riddles proposed by caretakers is the simpler, playful, manifest epiphenomenon of a more fundamental relation to the enigma of the other. A dialectical sequence is thereby initiated, for while the child was seen at first as passively subjected to the impact of the adult's message, it is now actively working to create meaning out of it, and then actively seeking for a renewed exposure to the enigma of the other. The epistemophilic drive is then in part responsible for the libidinal overtones of translation, in excess of the bare mechanics of a strictly cognitive process. I believe that this view resonates with Winnicott's description of the *joy* found in the object's survival.

The object, however, "is *in fantasy* always being destroyed" (UO, p. 93), and Winnicott also posits that "here fantasy begins for the individual" (p. 90). The expression "in fantasy" is shorthand for more complex matters requiring a few further remarks about translation. As the child tries to construe its meanings out of the impact of the enigmatic messages, it is elaborating a set of theories about the world and about itself. The word "theories" evokes the views of developmental psychologists who describe the child as a full-fledged "theorist" (Gopnik & Meltzoff, 1997), but it also refers to the classic Freudian "infantile sexual theories" and implies the primary level of theorizing which psychoanalysts call a "fantasy". Is not a fantasy, indeed, a scenario in which subject and object are put into motion for the attainment of a satisfactory goal? And is not a theory something that aims at describing how the world works and how one should go about the world in order to reach some satisfactory result? Theories, of course, are even more complex. We have theories about the world and theories about ourselves inside that world, and theories about how we theorize about the world. In other words, there is a representation of translation resulting from the very process of translation. Simply put, there is a self-theorizing agent elaborating a self-representation of himself-as-translator.[10]

The result is a superordinate level of translation, a decisive leap in the complexity of the child's mind. The fantasy of destroying the object precisely reflects this level of complexity. The object can be destroyed *in fantasy,* insofar as translation has reached the superordinate level of functioning where it is possible to treat both oneself *and* the object as belonging to the *same* category—that is, both are now *virtual objects,* the *result of the subject's translation: of its fantasy-making.*

I would go as far as saying that *fantasy formation itself is the actual form of destruction* meant by Winnicott. Destroying *in* fantasy equals destroying *by* fantasy, but this does not make it a less serious business. It must be stressed indeed that fantasy-making is not itself a fantasy; it is something real—that is, an actual accomplishment correlated with ongoing changes in the subject's attitude towards the other. There is some truth in the Italian proverb

"*Traduttore, traditore*" [a translator is always a traitor], and in this case we may add: and fortunately so (Scarfone, 1999). By constructing its own meanings, the child is destroying something of the earlier state of affairs, thereby strengthening its status as a subject. The object, if it is to survive this change, must accept such destruction, which is nothing else than the death of the "bundle" in which subject and object were indistinctly bound. The object must also welcome the subject's rejection of its former belief in the caretaker's unlimited power to influence its mind. When things evolve smoothly, the importance of this new phase in the subject–object relationship may not be apparent; it is more conspicuous when the object does not tolerate, let alone support, the child's strivings at autonomous thinking. This is most apparent, for instance, in the parent's reaction to the child's first lie (Scarfone, 1998), a major marker of the child's newly acquired sense of possessing a mind of its own.

To retaliate, then, means, among other things, for the object to oppose the subject's efforts at thinking by itself. It is to force the subject back into a state of submission to the literalness of the object's dictum (Scarfone, 2003). The relationship is then frozen, and the consequence for the child is that it cannot reach the liveliness and the feeling of being real to which Winnicott often referred in the later period of his life (Phillips, 1988).

5. "Subject can use object": the use of two authors

It is remarkable, in view of what I have proposed above, that at the end of his paper Winnicott does not state precisely what he means by "use", except to mention that he does not mean "exploitation". But Winnicott's minimalist definition is really congruent with the very process he has been describing. How indeed, when it comes to allowing for a creative way of relating to the object, could Winnicott positively describe—and thereby *prescribe*—the meaning of the verb "to use"? Would not that amount to a form of impingement? We then find ourselves in a position where Winnicott's text is also giving us permission to use it for our own benefit, in thinking by ourselves, insofar as our destroying is only potential and there is no anger in it. My personal use of Winnicott has here taken the form of a "translation" into the language of another author, Laplanche, who refers to translation itself as a paradigm for psychic differentiation and for the establishment of a subjective position with regard to the impact of the other.

Certainly, pursuing the project of bringing together two think- ers of such stature as Winnicott and Laplanche is a risky business, but my hope is that the steps described by Winnicott also apply to what I have done in this chapter. (1) I have indeed been *relating* to both Winnicott and Laplanche, possibly in a projective way. (2) By bringing them together I was forced to *discover* them in some new objective dimension. (3) I have probably been doing some kind of *destroying* of both of them by trying to elaborate a personal view about them. (4) It is to be hoped that both their theories have *survived* and that neither will retaliate or backfire! (5) If my experi- ment was well conducted, then I hope I have contributed, however slightly, to a meaningful *use* of Laplanche and Winnicott, as well as to opening some paths towards a creative debate among different psychoanalytic schools. Finally, I hope that despite its laborious course, this chapter was able to provide a measure of enjoyment in thinking about our discipline.

Notes

1. This is a simplification of the matter, however, as the adult is not really a centre either, being also de-centred by his or her own unconscious.

2. Such distinction is allowed by Winnicott's placing of transitional phe- nomena "between the oral eroticism and the true object relationship" ("Transi- tional Objects and Transitional phenomena", 1971g, p. 2). By way of logical deduction, since in "The Use of an Object" transitional phenomena occur after object-relating, the latter cannot be conflated with true object relationship.

3. Intention does not necessarily imply a self-reflexive level of mindedness, nor, for that matter, consciousness.

4. It must be noticed, in passing, that "to go on" is akin to Winnicott's "to go on being", although the latter expression refers to a more fundamental process.

5. This intricate dialectics, by the way, resolves an apparent anachronism in Winnicott's sequence: first relating to an object and then finding it! A common- sense approach would consider first finding and then relating. But accurate accounts of reality often run counter to common sense. If relating comes before finding the object, it is because Winnicott's description is consistent with the

view that at this stage, as we have seen, "relating to an object" implies no true distinction between subject and object.

6. Which is an idea present in Klein's concept of projective identification, but with a major difference: that here there is no separation between the projector and the recipient of the projections and no aim at controlling anything on the part of the projector.

7. The mother's face as a mirror has been described in another chapter of *Playing and Reality.*

8. Except by some entrapment in a perverse knot of recurrent, redundant translation, which is a case of serious psychopathology.

9. Laplanche has nevertheless indirectly touched upon this matter in another context, by noticing that creators are often "traumatophilic"—that is, they need renewed traumatic experiences to stimulate their creative work. This seems to me a specific case of the general view expressed here. On the other hand, one is also reminded that the impact of enigmatic message, even in its benign form, is always "traumatic" (Laplanche, 1980).

10. This is akin to what Freud (1900a), after Silberer, called the functional role of the dream, where the dream represents the inner state of the dreamer at the time of the dreaming.

CHAPTER FOUR

Childhood sexual theories and childhood sexuality: the primal scene and parental sexuality

Andreas Giannakoulas

Freud never abandoned the subject of sexuality, and it has by no means been neglected by child, adolescent, and adult analysts since. In this chapter my aim is to discuss a particular aspect of infantile fantasies and infantile sexuality and, in particular, how their development derives a substantial contribution from interaction with the parental couple's unconscious world. I shall first outline some basic contributions to the theme of the primal scene.

Freud writings between the beginning of 1905 and the end of 1926 constitute a "magnum opus", and throughout that work his insight was to perceive clearly the intimate connection between infantile sexuality and adult sexuality, and between the manifestations of early sexuality and the onset of neurosis and the perversions. The sequence of his brilliant clinical observations shows an increasing complexity and richness (something like an add-on process, but where what matters are the new links being established).

The description of Little Hans shows a small boy struggling through his feminine and masculine oedipal conflict, his love and hate, and his desire for knowledge. This might seem quite linear and self-evident, but Freud remarks that the compulsion to active knowledge, also found in Leonardo in his childhood years, "converted his passion into a thirst for knowledge" (1909b, p. 74). Just a few years later, the analysis of the Rat Man (1909d) revealed castration anxiety as a central anxiety, possibly connected with masturbation fantasies. With the Wolf Man (1918b [1914]), Freud showed how longer and deeper analytic work revealed a much more complex and powerful interaction between drives, object, and *phantasies*, and discovered that castration anxiety has to be related to phantasy configurations and the inference of a primal scene. This was worked out through the analysis of the Wolf Man's dream, and its representation of a reconstructed exposure to parental coitus at the age of 18 months. Through these texts, Freud's view of the oedipal complex acquires depth and complexity, and it also becomes linked with the primal fantasy itself as a configuration with multiple entries and unending transformations in the individual's development and *in the transference*.

The essential problem, as Freud saw it at that time (around 1910 to 1914) was the relationship of perversion to the Oedipus complex, to the unconscious, and to repression, and the task of reconciling some of the viewpoints of the *Three Essays* (1905d) with the ideas emerging from the later clinical material was rather difficult. In the *Three Essays*, Freud seems to regard perversion as "the negative of neurosis", as a more or less direct manifestation of component sexual instincts, scarcely capable of further reduction, and as a direct expression of the persistence of infantile sexuality. But, apart from their differences, there are also similarities between perversion and neurosis, for both are residues of the great developmental processes of infantile sexuality.

In "A Child Is Being Beaten" (1919e), Freud showed that the component instinct is not part of a straight continuum with perversion, because it must first pass through the Oedipus complex. This paper makes explicit that a particular perverse fantasy is unequivocally related to the Oedipus complex and to various forms of defence against it. Freud further suggests that the relationship to the Oedipus complex has a more general validity for all infantile sexuality and sexual deviations.

With the introjection of the parents and the dissolution of the complex, the child builds up, in the shape of the superego, the same barrier towards the drives which existed before in the external world *in the form of the parents*. But the superego is not the mere sum of parental identifications; it is a distinct structure, healthy or faulty, more or less archaic, *inside* the ego.

In 1926, Freud pointed out that as a result of the long period of helplessness and dependence of the human infant, "the influence of the real external world upon it is intensified and an early differentiation between the ego and the id is promoted" (1926d [1925], pp. 154–55). This raises the question of how the reality of the parents, which includes their psychic life as individuals and as a couple, can interact with and shape the emerging qualities of the child's phantasies.

This is a point that can be enriched by one of Ferenczi's seminal contributions, where he addresses this problem from an entirely new perspective. Indeed, he reverses the perspective, by raising the issue of the serious consequences a child can encounter when the adult interprets its need for tenderness in an erotic key (1933). This *confusion of tongues* is at the root of incestuous seduction. If the child is abused in the phase of tenderness, his or her fantasies are elevated to the level of reality, with the consequence that the child is forced to manage a precocious implantation of passionate love mingled with guilt. But even if *"more love or love of a different kind from that which they need* is forced upon the children . . . it may lead to pathological consequences in the same way as the *frustration or withdrawal of love* . . ." (p. 164). Thus, the child is deprived of his very need for tenderness, which is replaced either by a precocious erotization or by a similarly precocious ego development. This is a matter of the adult's needs leading to the abuse of the needs of the child.

According to Pontalis (1977):

> Ferenczi considered the *child as interiorizing adult desires* marked by hate, guilt and prohibition. Invoking his thesis at this point may seem paradoxical as it is already so surprising in itself, in as much as it aimed to bring back to life a Freudian conception previous to the discovery of infantile sexuality. By basing itself on seduction are we not poles apart from Melanie Klein? However, one should not be too hasty to assert that Ferenczi's thesis is no more than a new incarnation of the "old" Freudian theory of seduction. [p. 101, emphasis added]

Pontalis adds,

> What Ferenczi discovered in the privileged example of seduction was a process with far-reaching consequences: identification with the aggressor or, rather, with his introjection. [p. 101]

This again brings us to the issue of the emotional environment, and to the role of adult—that is, parental contributions to the shaping, expression, and elaboration of the child's sexuality and fantasies. This can be conveniently explored, from both a developmental and a psychopathological point of view, with the help of Paula Heimann, who concisely and effectively wrote about introjection: "When the ego receives stimuli from outside, it absorbs them and makes them part of itself, it introjects them . . . we can define the beginning of the ego with the first introjections of another psychological entity" (Heimann, 1952, p. 125).

The central point of this approach is made explicit by Laplanche (1987):

> Although Ferenczi raises the issue of the asymmetry in the relationship between the child and the adult, he avoids dealing with the problem of the parental unconscious. In fact, Ferenczi does not take into consideration that what he calls "language of passion" (the language of the adult), is traumatizing only to the extent to which it carries a meaning which is unknown even to himself, namely there where the presence of the parental unconsciousness manifests itself. [pp. 123–124, translated for this edition]

If we consider the problem from the child's viewpoint, this means his being often a symptom of the parental collusive unconscious, because of the weakness and dependency of the child's ego when confronted with the overwhelming power of early objects.

This theme was developed by those analysts who had been working with children and parents, in particular by Melitta Sperling, by Kolb and Johnson (1955), and by Sadger (1921), who, in Gillespie's words, "have drawn our attention to the way in which a faulty superego may be developed when the parental model interferes with normal development and treats pregenital or perverse activities with relative leniency, or even encourages them, because they fulfil an unconscious perverse need in the parent"

(1955, p. 85). Again, Sylvia Payne, in her acute observations on "the ego development of the fetishist", notes that, "The fetish therefore stands for part-objects which have been eaten and also preserved. The internalized objects may have the significance of pre-genital superego formations. . . . The relationship of a man to his fetish is the same as his relationship to his internalized parents" (Payne, 1939, p. 167).

It should also be noted that the characteristics and interrelations of inner object relationships are also fashioned by the characteristics of the parents. The vicissitudes of the internal objects, "parental images" within the ego and their externalization, and the "release" of the introjects have been described very aptly by Bychowski, Khan, Milner, and others. The significant point here, then, is that the relationship between internal objects not only implies a contribution from the parents' unconscious, but also that the child's fantasy of intimacy and separateness of those objects (i.e., the phantasy of the primal scene) has to come to terms with the parents' own unconscious fantasies of intimacy and separateness.

In referring to the work of Sigmund Freud and Melanie Klein, Paula Heimann provided us with the most concise summary of the repertoire of infantile sexuality, "unconscious equations", and those fantasies that Freud called "infantile sexual theories". She writes:

> To begin with, the infant knows only part-objects. . . . Only gradually does he achieve the integration of his multiple impressions and weave them into the recognition of persons . . . and [realize] that there is an interrelation between his parents. . . . Naturally the first stage differs in many respects from the climax, the "classical" Oedipus phase. . . . In addition to part-objects the incorporation fantasies now concern "whole" objects, the parents as persons, as complex entities with bewildering things going on between them. [1952, pp. 66–67]

Urges from the various bodily zones, with their dual sexual and destructive charge, operate towards the parents in both outer and inner worlds, leading to a wealth of conflicting and confusing emotions.

It is to this period of instinctual and conceptual confusion that we attribute the origins of the unconscious equations first pointed out by Freud and found in every analysis: between organs and substances, breast/penis, mouth/vagina, penis/faeces/babies, urine/milk, and so on. To mention these unconscious equations is tantamount to referring summarily to a great number of infantile fantasies that we have to regard as ubiquitous. Parental intercourse is the centre of these fantasies. Consequently, parental intercourse assumes the character of the "primal scene".

As we know "the primal scene" represents a fundamental fantasy pattern, a central representation about the nature of parental intercourse, around which defences, infantile fantasies and theories, often endowed with a peculiar traumatic and traumatogenic quality, are organized and which often reveal a compulsion to relive actively what once had to be endured passively. Today we would be more inclined to say that they are organizing a fantasy of being in omnipotent control of the internalized parents.

It was recognized that while the primal scene—in the original sense of the witnessing of parental intercourse or of some clearly related sexual event, such as birth or miscarriage—was not clearly remembered by the young child: it combined with impressions from related experiences to give rise to various infantile sexual theories. Subsequently, the most frequent emphasis was on the power of the fantasy of the primal scene, rather than on the actual experience. The term then shifted to refer especially to the fantasies, whether or not the actual experience had occurred.

Phyllis Greenacre develops her thought about the primal scene by starting from the recognition of three concurrent determinants: the witnessing by the child of parental sexual intercourse or of some "clearly related sexual event"; the child's contribution in terms of a changing, interwoven bundle of reciprocally shaping perceptions, impressions, distortions, illusions, fantasies, and theories concerning the nature of the parent's intimate, secluded, exciting relationship; the parents' reactions and responses to the child's fantasized or actual intrusion. She writes:

> I believe such experiences to be ubiquitous, and the starting point of potent fantasies. The conditions at the time of the experience often influence the reactions to later events and so shape the theories that gradually develop throughout childhood. The direct, seemingly not elaborated memory, if pre-

sented at all, is usually updated to a later time. On analysis it proves to be a screen memory with distortions and discrepancies. If it is held to with great vehemence and thin rationalizations, it becomes an illusion, often in striking contrast to the individual's good sense of reality in the ordinary affairs of life. It is dislodged by analysis against great resistance. Derivative parts of the original experiences usually appear in the dreams, screen memories, behaviour and symptoms of later life, and especially in the fantasies associated with masturbation. [Greenacre, 1973, p. 11]

Winnicott seems to find a truly new, *fertile* perspective when he affirms in *Human Nature* that parental sexuality has a more complex meaning. The main by-product of confronting himself with the primal scene,

when parents actually exist, is the sorting out of what is called reality and fantasy. . . . The sexual union of father and mother provides a fact, a hard fact around which the child can build a fantasy, a rock to which he can cling and against which he can kick; and furthermore it provides part of the natural foundation for a personal solution of the triangular relationship. . . . The primal scene (parents together sexually) is the basis of individual stability since it makes possible the whole dream of taking the place of one partner. . . . Seeing the parents together makes the dream of their separation, or of the death of one of them, tolerable. [1988, p. 59]

Winnicott expressed his debt to Freud, who

did a great deal of the work for us . . . putting forward the importance of instinct and the significance of childhood sexuality. . . . Almost every aspect of relationships between whole persons was touched on by Freud himself, and in fact it is very difficult now to contribute except by fresh statement of what is accepted. Any theory that denies or bypasses these matters is unhelpful. [1988, p. 36]

But, in Winnicott's view, instincts serve the self; they do not constitute it. He states that "It is the self that must precede the self's use of instinct." Winnicott describes the problem very succinctly in his earlier, unpublished *Didactic Statement on Child Development* of 1962, and I will quote him in full:

By psycho-analytic theory we see boys and girls of toddler age engaged in experiencing and coping with instinctual drives of maximum strength. There are the two patterns, the triangle in which the parent of the opposite sex is loved and the one the same sex hated, and the inverted Oedipus complex in which the homosexual attachment holds sway. The child in the family has a good chance in the course of the years—shall we say 2– 5—of getting enough experience in both patterns to be able to go on to the latency period with a feeling of relief: I've had it, and now I can do with a rest from instinctual growth and all that entails.

As you know only too well, the trouble with the instinctual life is that it needs whole-time management. The child that is healthy suffers from acute anxiety attacks in this period of most intense feeling associated with excitement in the excitable parts of the body. The healthy child of this age is often angry and often in despair, even depersonalized when excitement goes over into a phase of slow detumescence (if I may use this word to cover more than the physical state). The instinctual life of the child involves him and her in conflicts that are insoluble, and hate that cannot be either endured or expressed, as well as leading to the experiencing of the prototypes of all subsequent loving, the loving of adolescent and adult life.

The child's most intense experiences are in fantasy, or rather in the child's personal inner psychic reality of which fantasy is a surface phenomenon. And these intense experiences involve the deepest layers, the layers that have direct access to consciousness, and which reach back to the child's earliest examples of instinctual experience.

Without the Oedipus complex psycho-analysis could not have been founded, because it is the most difficult area in the emotional growth of healthy persons, and we ought not to do the treatment of persons who are disturbed at stages prior to that of the Oedipus conflict unless when we get them forward we can carry them over the Oedipal conflicts when they arise in the transference.

You know for instance that a great deal of development has taken place before a child is able to experience anything so healthy as an Oedipus complex, which involves a relationship between the child as a whole person and two other persons perceived as whole.

Also you know that Ego integration is the term that lies conveniently to hand when we think of the structure and dynamic cohesiveness that is needed if a child is not only to survive this phase but also have it in his other pocket for use at puberty and after.

It may be useful to show a lively clinical application of this statement in Winnicott's reference to the primary scene in his clinical encounter with the little girl, Gabrielle, the "Piggle". Since he was very aware of the intrusive inadequacy of language in child analysis, he formulated his interpretations with measured economy and did not immediately verbalize the sexual elements. The growth of the relationship between him and Gabrielle is crucial for a deep interpretation of his that is verbalized with deliberate informality.

> If you were a man, you would push your wee-wee into the hole which the skirt covers.
>
> Gabrielle: Do you know I'm going to have some apple juice in the train? Daddy said we must remember to bring back some for Susan.
>
> Me: You feel a bit frightened to really have me all to yourself. When you have me or daddy alone you have the wee-wee going in and making babies, and so you don't have to go at it and get out the stuff that's inside it, so you don't feel so awful about that, but then you feel Susan will be jealous because it's so good.
>
> . . . I interpreted that she was showing me she could put two people together, and she could get in between daddy and mummy to join or separate them, and that would be three. But it was more than she could do to fit in Susan too—a fourth didn't fit in. This seemed all right. [1977, p. 158]

To my knowledge, this is one of the most explicit interpretations of child sexuality recorded in psychoanalysis. Many levels are addressed at the same time: oedipal and pre-oedipal conflicts, genital and pregenital fantasies and functioning, whole-object and part-object relationships. Freud's contribution is integrated with the British object-relations tradition and with Rickman's concept of one-, two-, three-, four-body relationships. This interpretation re-states in lively terms Freud's intuition that the birth of *another* baby elicits a new desire for knowledge and builds up curiosity towards a new area of inner affects, drives, and interpersonal relations. The reference to the parents is inevitable.

As a result of surviving the infant's and child's excited states, the "good-enough" parental couple allows the healthy child to become

> capable of the full dream of genital sexuality. This is composed of a *remembered dream* (subject to the dream work, censorship, displacement, condensation, etc.) and of an *"unremembered and unending dream*, in which the full consequences of the instinctual experience must be met. [1980, p. 58]

That is, the child has to go through the whole configuration of oedipal wishes and their consequences in fantasy. In Winnicott's words:

> The idea of the death of the father and therefore of his own death. The idea of castration by the father, or castration of the father. The idea of being left with full responsibility for the satisfaction of the mother. The idea of a compromise with the father, along homosexual lines. [1988, p. 59]

In the girl's dream, she cannot avoid dealing with an analogous predicament.

Ogden (1989) refers to the term "primal scene phantasy" as

> a group of conscious and unconscious phantasies on the theme of observed parental intercourse. These phantasies are characterized by varying degrees of primitivity, a range of modes of object relatedness, different forms and intensities of identification with each of the figures in the phantasy, and so on. [p. 142]

He maintains, further, following Winnicott, that

> The primal scene phantasy in its role as organizer of evolving sexual meaning and identity is by no means a static entity. Rather, it is a constellation of thoughts and feelings in which the form of object relatedness, the degree of subjectivity, the modes of defence, and the maturity and complexity of affect are all in a state of evolution and flux. The image of observed parental intercourse serves as a mold, a way of thinking about the unthinkable. [p. 149]

In a recent paper, Silvio Zucconi (2003) writes:

The primal scene phantasies (or *early body memories*) are the traces contained in the "black box" of the mind, which tells about the way the child has experienced parental sexuality (an entanglement of real perception and oneiric elaborations), during the various vicissitudes that characterize the individuation–separation processes and the construction of bodily ego and sexual identity.

Often, in child analysis, the play material could contain elements and features of the unending and unremembered dream of sexuality and, by not being remembered, may represent, in itself, a sort of playground in which the fantasies can be explored safely. Healthy children's sexual theories owe much more to the unremembered than to the remembered dream of sexuality. What is most important in Winnicott's discourse is that sexuality has to be worked through and released in dream—that is, through a dialogue and integration between different parts of the self, the increasing integration of excited and quiet experiences has to be transformed into a meaningful narrative.

Of course, the therapeutic process depends on an understanding of the symbolic edifice and of the symbol-generating processes that, in Winnicott's work with children, are translated not so much into the syntax of speech, but into the mutuality of the play. It is just this distance, this close presence of the known but unstated, that gives to play its intensity, its matchless energy of internal life where the imaginative contribution of the child is much more explicit and significant than any vocabulary available to him.

At this point, in order to understand the role that infantile sexuality and sexual fantasies play in the parental relation, it is necessary to say a few words about the child within the adult, and the fantasies and feelings that form part of the marvellous grasp of human particularity that is adult love. In falling in love, as in play, the area of imagination and illusion both unites and separates the couple.

The partners seek and find themselves in the other, subjectifying each other. In this potential space, neither is exclusively internal or external to the other. Both are located in an intermediate area of experience that sustains the interrelationship. "The re-finding of the object" gives to the object an unmistakable potentiality, conveying an energy of undeclared content which is felt, registered, as if it were present. In love, the free play of imaginative remembrance is immensely more explicit than any adult vocabulary available to the lovers and gives to what is experienced an unmistakable vitality, freshness, and playful recreation. By including the elements of play, the internal world and external reality could come together. The potentiality of the area of illusion exists in the possibility of the infinitely variable exchange of playing and intimacy where, through imaginatively shared sexual activities and through mobilizing body-interest, sexual fantasies can be dramatized and words, phrases, carnal exactitude, and externalization can be shared unvoiced, kept numinous for occasions of utter intimacy and initiation.

The search for infantile regression and for the gratification of infantile fantasies remain deep drives in adult sexuality. A special task is allocated to the ego's strength in managing greater regression with fewer anxieties. So in adult love the sense of mutual trust and reliability may produce a greater sense of security, autonomy, free desire, and the inevitability of the search for joint regression to more archaic levels in the wish to achieve profound mutual orgasm. This includes the imaginative elaboration of bodily parts and of the sensations and functions of the self in relation to the other. These become richer through new content and through regressive pregenital recuperations that include the primal scene. In consequence, there can be a capacity to seek, in sex, fulfilment of deeper infantile fantasies even from primary oral levels where the boundaries of the ego are least clear and the sense of identity and fusion with the partner is most complete. Satisfying sexual experiences serve also to regress to infantile levels and make it possible for the couple to have conscious and unconscious experience of the infantile wish for an illusory, perfect, primary love.

Most of children's unconscious representations of their bodies and their genitals will reflect the libidinal and narcissistic significance that the parents themselves imprint upon their child's physical and psychological self, as well as the extent to which they transmit their unconscious individual or shared fantasies concerning their own bodily and sexual functions. Often the unintegrated repressed or dissociated sexual components and the unresolved oedipal and pre-oedipal conflicts in the parental relationships create the space for a wide range of pathogenic and pathogenetic parental behaviour.

The importance of collusive parental conflicts as a possible factor in the aetiology or perpetuation of a child's illness has been touched on and suggested as an area for investigation by several researchers, such as Felix Deutsch, Vaughan and Cashmore, Milner, Balint, Lask, Winnicott, and Khan. The analytic situation—transference and countertransference, projective identification and counter-identification, the role given to the analyst, and so forth—and our work with parents and children, afford opportunities for gaining insight into some of the factors that may exacerbate the engagement in the normality and the pathology of others, as in the pathological collusions and massive projections in marriage that lead to driving the other mad. Difficulty in differentiating the "self" from the "other" and modifying infantile fantasies can create a situation where children can become involved and often used. The cross currents of projections and introjections in the couple could create and maintain shared pathological infantile fantasies and mutual blind distortions with constant misinterpretations, with resultant massive intrusions into the psychic space and body of the child. When the marital relationship is "a vehicle of primitive projections rather than a collaborative endeavour" (Sutherland, 1963, p. 64), the child's task of integrating adequately the emerging sexuality, depending on age and stage of development, becomes difficult, almost impossible.

Excessive and archaic defences against the disturbing parental sexuality could lead to inertia, apathy, lack of curiosity, and vitality in the child. In ill-health, according to Winnicott, the routes of the unremembered dream are either banned or dissociated, and often forced into reacting and acting out.

I think that in *Playing and Reality*, Winnicott added something quite new when he distinguished between fantasy and fantasying: "Fantasying remains an isolated phenomenon, absorbing energy but not contributing-in either to dreaming or to living" (1971a, p. 26).

Child sexuality was considered by early psychoanalysis only from an instinctual viewpoint. Further contributions have shown the rich interplay between parental environment and sexual development, but Phyllis Greenacre's very valuable work on "the primal scene", together with Winnicott's original views on the maturational instinctual and emotional emergent processes and faculties in the infant and the influence of early object relations, add a particular theoretical and clinical interest to the factors that enable the child to integrate a personal body-ego and psyche.

Note

This chapter is a translation and adaptation of A. Giannakoulas, "Teorie sessuali infantili e della sessualità infantile in relazione alla scena primaria e alla sessualità genitoriale". *Richard e Piggle,* Vol. 8, No. 1 (2000), pp. 16–24 (Rome: Il Pensiero Scientifico Editore).

CHAPTER FIVE

Violence and creativity

Joyce McDougall

V iolence and creativity? This may appear to be an odd coupling, so perhaps my theme requires some explanation before turning to its illustration. Let us begin by considering violence. The world around us appears increasingly violent in recent decades: accounts of genocide, religious persecution, racial purification, torture, and terrorism fill our papers and our television screens daily. Although the perpetrators attempt to justify their death-dealing acts on historical or religious grounds, the horror appears senseless—violence for violence's sake. Is it true, as is frequently asserted, that mankind has become more violent, more murderous than in former centuries? Or is it simply that the means of communication and information are more immediate and rapid than they were, so that we are now more directly faced with man's inhumanity to man. No journalists were there to report on Genghis Khan's ruthless course of conquest and domination as he swept over the Mongolian plains, nor were there any CNN cameramen then to film the slaughtering of every man, woman and child in Baghdad, when that city had defied him. And what of Carthage and the Roman vengeance, which even sought to destroy all future life by sowing the soil with salt? Man's inhumanity to man needs no emphasis. There is little doubt that human beings have always demonstrated the capacity for destroying other humans without a trace of guilt or remorse.

Humankind is not basically good; it may be more accurate to say that we are basically evil and that civilization is a triumphant achievement over our inherently barbarous and brutal nature. However, one of the aims of this chapter is to explore the notion that violence is not necessarily destructive: that it can also be constructive and creative—that man is indeed "an animal that builds cathedrals". This brings me to what is included in the notion of creativity and, eventually, then to the role of violence in the creative process.

For a number of years I have attempted to understand the mysterious origins of innovative expression in my analysands in whatever form this may take: whether expressed in writing, painting, sculpture, music, the performing arts, or in scientific and intellectual creativity, or creativity in the world of politics, business, and industrial invention. All these forms of creativity are connected with what Freud referred to as sublimations, activities that, although derived from the libidinal drives, have been deflected to another goal, one that is endowed with value in the eyes of society.

However, apart from those creators in whom the violence and transgression that are inherent to the creative process have caused suffering and breakdown, I shall also take into consideration those whose violence may be turned back upon their own selves, giving rise to symptomatic constructions. Therefore, to the socially esteemed activities I would like to add many other "creations" that do not have this social value: psychological symptoms, sexual deviations, psychotic manifestations, and psychosomatic illness. Although these phenomena do not qualify as sublimations, they nevertheless are creations of the self and, as such, have been constructed in the service of psychic survival. It is my contention that psychological symptoms and sublime creations all spring from the same source: the attempt to deal with early psychic conflict and primitive forms of mental pain. Some of these archaic psychic dramas are part and parcel of the universal traumata of human life: the existence of otherness, the discovery of the difference between the sexes, the inevitability of death. Then to these must be added the bi-parental unconscious, which may hold traumatic potential, and atypical traumata, such as the untimely death of a parent, psychosis in a family member, being brought into the world to replace a dead child, or living through a socially traumatic period.

The creative artist

From its inception, psychoanalysis has been fascinated by the mysteries of the creative process. In his essay "Creative Writers and Day-dreaming" (1908e [1907]), Freud writes: "From what sources does that strange being (the creative writer) draw his material?" He then goes on to suggest that *children at play* behave like a writer in that they create a world of their own. However, later in this same essay, he makes the surprising statement: "as people grow up they *cease to play*" and realize that they are expected "not to go on playing or phantasying any longer". This somewhat critical attitude towards fantasy and play in adulthood appears throughout Freud's writings, as though fantasies, and even the enjoyment of looking at paintings that fascinated him, were a guilty preoccupation. I remember, for example, reading in one of Freud's letters, I think to Fliess, "I have to confess that I once again succumbed to the charms of Da Vinci's painting." Furthermore, in the same paper on creative writing, Freud adds, "We may lay it down that a happy person never phantasizes, only an unsatisfied one."

Ongoing psychoanalytic research into the creative processes continued with Winnicott, who proposed a more optimistic view of fantasy, play, and creativity. Winnicott began his research in this area of human experience with the postulate of what he called "primary creativity": when a mother is absent or does not immediately comply with what her baby wants or needs, there is pain and puzzlement, which is then followed by fear and anger. Yet, as Winnicott intuitively proposed, this is the moment when infants get a first inkling of the knowledge that they and the maternal source of life are not one and indivisible. This, he proposes, is the earliest origin of becoming an "individual"—that is, a being who can no longer be divided into two defused parts, him or herself, and the Other. The infant, on the way to individuation, then sets about recreating in hallucinatory fashion the lost fusion with the maternal universe. Winnicott designates this hallucinatory pleasure the infant's earliest creative activity. Here, creation always has an aura of hallucination and illusion to fill what might otherwise be a frightening void.

Winnicott then came to conceptualize the phenomenon that he named "transitional space", in which both the inner and the outer world participate. He emphasizes that this potential space "widens out into that of play, and of artistic creativity and appreciation, and of religious feeling, and of dreaming" (1971g, p. 5). Thus, among the many factors that contribute to creativity, it could be said that the creator (in whatever field) is also playing. Here, in spite of their divergences, Freud and Winnicott share a similar vision. At this point, it is also worth recalling Winnicott's statement regarding the practice of psychoanalysis as a creative pursuit. He claimed that it was essential that the psychoanalyst could allow his or her own imagination and fantasy life to flow freely during the work with analysands. And he further emphasized that "If the analyst cannot play, he is not suitable for the work" (1971c, p. 54).

I would like to add at this point that this playful dimension to creativity does not mean that it is *carefree*. On the contrary, my analysands have taught me that their originative activity is frequently pursued in a spirit of rage, desperation, and sometimes of depression. But here again, the metaphor of the creator as a child at play is most pertinent. Children do not limit their play to enacting the wish to be magical or to possess the privileges of their parents; they also use playing to overcome experiences that have been frightening or traumatic. The little girl who has just come back from the dentist will play at brutally drilling her doll's teeth, or she may ask her playmate to be the patient while she enacts the role of the dentist. In this way, the experience of pain and fear in situations in which one had no mastery is playfully discharged in a game where the victim becomes the victimizer. This was first grasped as a vital part of human experience by Freud in his account of the infant with the cotton reel. Freud was watching one of his small grandchildren whose mother had gone out, and the little child kept throwing the cotton reel over the side of his cot and then making it come back, shouting "Fort-da" with evident excitement. In other words, he was no longer the victim of the mother's absence but the master symbolically of the disappearance and the subsequent reappearance.

I would like to suggest that in the course of analysis with creative people we find similar processes at work. Many years of working with children in psychotherapy have helped me to understand in my adult patients the factors that underlie the urgent need to create, as well as giving me some insight into the factors that *inhibit* creativity. Such analysands usually turn to psychoanalysis at a time when their creativity is painfully blocked, for reasons that, in general, they do not understand. A certain number of my patients have taught me that their innovative activity, while it arouses excitement and satisfaction, also frequently brings in its wake intense feelings of transgression, anguish, and guilt. The resistance to continuing with one's work is a common experience to many a creative worker, particularly in the plastic arts and the field of literary and scientific writing. And indeed, I have observed that this resistance is sometimes most acutely experienced when the creator feels intensely inspired by a pristine vision, invention, or idea that is clamouring for expression. I shall attempt to explain later why this should be so.

Violence as a foundation stone of psychic structure

Melanie Klein emphasized, more incisively than any other psychoanalytic writer of the time, the importance of violent emotion and its role in structuring the substratum of the human psyche. In advancing the notion that artistic creativity was linked to the turbulent relations between infant and mother, she threw new light upon the inner world of the creative being. Klein, of course, tended to attribute creative blockage to a lack of integration of the infant's envy and destructiveness towards the breast-mother. While this may be one contributory factor, many other factors, to which I shall return later, appear to be equally important. Nevertheless, Klein's perspective has interested me in that clinical observation and reflection have led me to conclude that violence is an essential element in all creative productions, including, as already mentioned, the construction of psychological and psychosomatic symptoms. Apart from the force and intensity of the creative urge, innovative individuals are indeed intrinsically violent, to the extent that they exercise their power to *impose* their thought, image, dream, or nightmare on other individuals in the external world.

In the course of the analytic voyage, my analysands and I have frequently uncovered the feeling that, in being creative, one is transgressing an invisible taboo, as though engaged in an activity that is either forbidden or extremely dangerous. The case of Bénédicte, extensively explored in *The Many Faces of Eros* (McDougall, 1995), is a pristine example of these internal and unconscious conflicts that may cause artistic paralysis. In the light of these analytic experiences, I have come to understand some of the reasons for which anxiety and mental pain are so frequently experienced in relation to creative production. In the analytic voyage with creative analysands, I feel that I have been presented with a privileged insight into the factors that contribute to creative activity as well as the unconscious fantasies that inhibit it and lie behind the sudden failure to create.

The world of internal violence

I have proposed in my writing that we might envisage the internal universe of the creative personality as similar to a volcano, a subterranean space that is churning with energy and that sends out sparks, rocks, and flames when it reaches the point of needing to eject the elements that are part of its very being. However, if this violent dispersion into the external atmosphere were to be blocked, it would eventually cause an immense and possibly life-endangering explosion. To my mind, the creative drive unconsciously resembles such a continuing source of energy that demands release. In this connection, it is pertinent to remark that the majority of creative people, in whatever field, are astonishingly productive. The feverish pressure to produce—the compulsion to create—is a vital element in the understanding of those analysands who come to us because of a blockage in their work. This enables us to empathize with their extreme tension, as well as identifying with the depression that accompanies their paralysed creativity.

To come back to the theme of violence in the creative act, I would like to reproduce a small extract from the letter of an exanalysand who had come to analysis because she could not allow herself to paint in the way she longed to do. The letter is quoted in full in *The Many Faces of Eros*, but since I have her permission to use her remarks for a scientifically oriented audience, I am turning to this source once again. Some years after the end of the analysis that had enabled her to become a well-known Parisian painter, she wrote the following lines, summing up what she had learned from her analysis with regard to the creative process:

> The profound primordial drives that surge up in me can become powerful enough to cause discomfort; the constant build up of tension has to be put outside of me, into the outer world in order to restore some feeling of harmony inside. It is creation, but it is fired by feelings of destruction. When I cannot paint, I become the target of my own violent aggression.
>
> I understand so well the frustration of my dear friend Jacques A, who says he hates his paintings because "they never depict the painting he has in his mind". Then there is Pierre B . . . who periodically destroys every painting he still has in his studio. Is this what Freud called the "death instinct"?

It may be recalled that Freud derived the theory of the death impulses from the libido itself. I sometimes feel that the name he gave to this concept of a "death instinct" might have been better translated as the "anti-life force". In any case, Freud shocked the intellectual world of Vienna when he announced that mankind, far from having one predominant desire—that of enjoying life and seeking love, pleasure, and narcissistic satisfaction—had an equally strong primordial tendency to self-destruction and a tendency to do everything in its power to destroy the possibility of making life pleasurable and rewarding. We all recognize this anti-life force for certain periods of time in our analysands, and, if we are honest, in ourselves also!

Experience has led me to appreciate that this drive towards self-destruction may be looming in the background of any creative activity. Feelings of depression, self-hatred, anger, and frustration, leading to a wish to destroy the work in progress, are often encountered. I have come to the notion that creative and innovative activity, among its many other aims, also serves, unconsciously, to heal the drive to destruction of oneself and/or others, and thus overcome feelings of fragmentation and disorientation. Creative

individuals, without being consciously aware of it, are often dealing with fragmented parts of themselves that urgently seek and
need to find a sense of individuality and cohesion through their
created works or inventions.

This reflection calls to mind my impressions on visiting, in
France, an important retrospective of the works of the two British
artists, Francis Bacon and Lucien Freud, both remarkable painters
whose violence is communicated directly to those who look at
these striking ways of portraying human beings. I noted a remark
of Bacon's quoted in the exhibition catalogue, in which he explained that he could never paint from a live model: he required
photographs, rough sketches, and so on—because (I quote from the
French catalogue), "the violent destruction that I must visit upon
my model is so great, so hateful, that I would find it difficult to
continue with my painting in his presence". Lucien Freud, on the
other hand, claimed that he required his model to be constantly
present, so that he would not lose the sense of the intrinsic quality
of each particular person whose portrait engaged his interest.

Erotogenic origins of the creative act

Following on from Winnicott's concept of primary creativity, I
would now like to summarize my thoughts concerning the importance of pregenital eroticism in the creative processes. It is clear
that pregenital sexuality draws its importance and richness from
the fact that it involves all five senses as well as all bodily functions.
However, as we well know, certain senses, erogenous zones, and
bodily functions are often unconsciously experienced as forbidden
sources of pleasure or as activities that are potentially dangerous
and violent.

The very fact of taking into one's body and mind impressions
received through any of the five senses is a creative act in itself. The
innovator or creator in any field is inevitably inspired by something in the external world, and once these impressions, perceptions, and thoughts are mentally incorporated, they fertilize the
inner psychic reality of the creative mind. However, this perpetual
movement between the two worlds, inner and outer, can be expe-

rienced and feared as an orally devouring or destructive act, and this immediately suggests that there may have been a breakdown in the maturational phase of transitional phenomena.

I have referred elsewhere (McDougall, 1995) to a portrait painter who frequently destroyed portraits that were highly important to him. In the many years of our analytic voyage, we discovered that, in a megalomanic and childlike way, he held himself responsible for his mother's partially paralysed face, which, in his unconscious fantasy, he had orally attacked and devoured with his mouth and his eyes. In a sense he had spent his life trying to repair the catastrophic damage caused by his infantile oral projections. His portraits were explosive attacks upon the visual world and yet, at the same time, were reparative in that they restored a striking likeness to the individual portrayed. While I am totally ignorant of the inner psychic world of painters such as Francis Bacon, I can readily imagine that his creations are partially inspired and fired by similar fears of archaic affects and the need to externalize this primitive source of internal violence. His remark concerning his need to protect his portrait models from the "attacks" he will be obliged to make upon their image would appear to confirm this hypothesis. But I must reiterate that while these dimensions do not explain the mysteries of creativity, they do help us to understand the phases of paralysis and inability to continue producing that arise in creative individuals.

I have also used elsewhere the statements of an inventive plastic surgeon who claimed that his mother was an unusually ugly woman. His self-denigration on the few occasions when his work was not impeccably successful enabled us to uncover the unconscious fantasy that he himself had rendered his mother ugly. By means of a highly original surgical invention, he was able to invest, creatively, the same violence he had experienced in his early relationship to his mother. Once, when he was faced with what he considered to be unfair criticism from other medical specialists, he said (I am translating from the French), "But they're so unfair— after all, I cut *to cure*." In deconstructing this phrase we learned that, through cutting, he satisfied a number of different pregenital drives, while at the same time making reparation for his fantasized destructiveness. From there on, he was able to accept further criticism from doubtlessly envious colleagues, without its causing him sleepless nights and an immense anger he found difficult to discharge.

Then again, the act of giving something of oneself to the external world may also be unconsciously equated with defecation and therefore a source of potential humiliation. In this respect, I would like to refer briefly to a clinical vignette taken from a case quoted more fully in *The Many Faces of Eros*. Tamara was a talented violinist, and a prize-winning pupil of the Paris Conservatory, who suffered such paralysing anxiety before a performance that she sometimes had to cancel her engagements at the last minute. After many months of mutual research, in which we attempted to reconstruct the unconscious scenario that was being enacted before every anticipated concert, she was able to capture the following fantasy: "I fool the whole world. Everybody will see that all I produce is shit, and that I myself am as valueless as a pile of shit".

Some months later she said: "You know I've never realized this before, but one of the reasons I wanted so badly to learn the violin when I was a little girl was because I thought it had a 'female silhouette'." From there on she began to think of her violin as an extension of her own body and realized that this was one inhibitory factor since it was forbidden to show her erotically tinged feminine body to the public. During her analytic adventure, she learned for the first time to love and caress her body without terror that it might bring down mortal punishment upon her, for she had been severely punished for masturbating at a very young age. These insights had a dramatic effect upon her wish to play in public.

With the new investment of her bodily being, she began to explore other unconscious fantasies that she had attached to all of her body's natural functions. At one session she announced, "You know, you have led me to understand that there is 'good shit' and 'bad shit'. Why can I not accept that I want to offer good things to the public?" Beneath her fear that she would exhibit what she believed to be an ugly and sexless body, there was also a desire to drown the whole world, father and mother, in murderous faeces. Tamara slowly began to live in her body and to enjoy its erotic potentiality, and this eventually enabled her to understand that she had valuable gifts to offer to the outside world. As she expressed it: "I need to feel erotically violent as I take my violin into my arms.

Nowadays I stroke it with passion which produces a much greater depth of sound than I ever achieved before when all I was permitted to do was to stroke it gently in order to avoid offending or hurting anybody."

The analytic voyage with analysands like Tamara has shown me the extent to which artistic creation originates from the erotogenic body of infancy and derives much of its force—as well as its frailty—from the way in which the creator's body was libidinally and narcissistically invested in the early bi-parental relationship. Although these profound libidinal and narcissistic drives are the primal source of the overwhelming urge to create, the psychic possession of one's emotions of anger and rage is equally vital to creative production.

Thus the medium—whether it be paint, marble, words, the voice, the body, a musical instrument, or a social or political institution—will always present itself as both an ally and an enemy. The medium has to be "tamed" so that the creator can impose his or her will upon it, while at the same time feeling convinced that it has the power to transmit to the outer world the message, vision, or new concept.

But creators and innovators frequently feel they must engage in a violent struggle with the outside world in order to obtain the right to display the most intimate expressions of their inner universe. The relationship between the creative personality and the anonymous public is a love affair that bristles with hazards. Of course, as analysts we are first concerned to understand what exactly is projected upon this public. Is it felt to be appreciative, desirous of receiving the creative offer, or, on the contrary, persecutory and rejecting? Creative artists in the course of their analytic voyage begin to find words to express what they have unconsciously believed would be the impact of their production or invention upon the anonymous partner, the public. These projections are indelibly marked by pregenital drives in which archaic sexual fantasies play a cardinal role. Although these are permeated with oral, anal, and phallic fantasies, the faecal and anal components occupy a special place. The faecal object is the first "creation" that the infant offers to the external world. But in addition to being the source of the earliest exchange between infant and mother, faecal and anal drives are also charged with violent fantasies of both an erotic and a sadistic nature. The anal product is a gift of great value offered with love, but at the same time it is frequently experienced as a violent production intended to attack and dominate one's significant objects in the external world. Furthermore, in contradistinction to oral and genital drives, the anal impulses and their faecal expressions are forcibly subjected to control with regard to their spontaneous expression, and therefore they have to be sublimated or in other ways deflected from their original, object-related aspects. So we may readily understand that the anal-erotic and anal-sadistic drives involved in creative production may provide an important determinant to the creator's capacity or incapacity to continue producing.

Before concluding, I would like to refer briefly once again to the significance of the universal bisexual wishes of infancy insofar as the creative processes are concerned. Infants normally identify with both parents and want to possess the privileges and magic powers of each for themselves, and these are usually symbolized by the parents' sexual organs. To the extent that the masculine and the feminine parts of every individual are well integrated and accepted, we all have the potentiality to be creative, to sublimate, so to speak, the impossible wish to be both sexes and to create children with both parents. This resolution may then permit us to produce parthenogenetic "infants" in the form of creative productions. But taking psychic possession of one's rights in this sense is also a violent act of introjection and identification. A little like one's liberty, it cannot be handed over with permission: one must seize it and take possession of it for oneself. This hypothesis adds weight to the proposition that there is no creative act or innovative thought that is not unconsciously experienced as an act of violence and transgression: One has dared to play alone, through one's chosen medium of expression, in order to fulfil secret libidinal, sadistic, and narcissistic aims; one has dared to display the resulting product to the whole world; in addition, one has dared to exploit pregenital sexuality, with all its attendant ambivalence; finally, one has dared, in unconscious fantasy, to "steal" the parents' generative organs and powers and, with these, proceeded to make one's own creative offspring. Small wonder that many potentially creative people do not create anything, and that those who do are frequently threatened from within by potential blockage.

In conclusion, I would propose that the very traumas that have most affected our psychosexual organization, and the violent affects and fantasies that such experiences have engendered in us, are a primal source not only of neurotic symptoms, inhibitions, or psychotic or psychosomatic breakdown, but of creativity itself.

CHAPTER SIX

Adult eros in D. W. Winnicott

Helen Taylor Robinson

In this study I argue that Winnicott's work on transitional objects and transitional phenomena in the life of the infant offers a formulation of some of the features of adult Eros, the mature fulfilment of genital sexuality between male and female.

I explore this by making use of Winnicott's observations of infancy in "Transitional Objects and Transitional Phenomena" (1971g) and in "The Use of an Object and Relating through Identifications" (1971h). The paper on "The Observation of Infants in a Set Situation" (1941) and the seven papers comprising "The Use of an Object" (1989) are assumed as background support for the general approach.

The movement from infantile to adult and the achievement of sublimation in adult sexuality will be addressed with reference to John Donne's poem "The Good-Morrow" (1633). The psychological and the poetic frames of reference are seen as complementary here in that there are no means to represent adult mature sexuality as a psychological phenomenon, even in statistical or clinical research studies, since the person with a mature sexual relationship does not seek the psychological analysis of this condition. Poets and other artists, however, by written reference to what is painful, difficult, and resistant to full maturity and to what embodies fulfil-ment and creativity, allow some exploration of what may occur in adult intercourse. The compression of language and the formal stylistic determinants of poetry express the complexity of such phenomena in a way that psychological analysis can never do. We *need* artistic insight to provide us with these references for psychic well-being.

Psychological—and, in particular, psychoanalytic—analysis proceeds in words, one aspect at a time. Art, through metaphor, condenses many matters at once. Though it may originate from and seek to address such human states, psychological analysis does not primarily communicate by means of intuition and emotion. But art depends on its ability to affect our feelings and thereby transform our understanding. In speaking the language of the psyche, rather than using language to infer, define, and refer to the psyche, artistic approaches are sensory *representations and embodiments* of distinct psychic phenomena, rather than ways of making indirect reference to them. These differences of aim and function are significant, and they indicate how we have to "make do" as we struggle with the inherent difficulties of psychic phenomena.

The different contributions of psychoanalytic and of poetic un-derstanding of representations of Eros, from its rudimentary fea-tures in infancy to its adult manifestation, will be significant to my argument. Eros will be taken to represent love in its sensual, erotic, possessive, desiring, attaching, affectionate, and devotional sense, primarily in the full relations between man and woman. I take the attainment of love to represent part of the achievement of a full relationship to reality, and a recognition of the phenomenon of loss. That is, the capacity for mature and generative sexual rela-tions includes the continuing redress of loss and sustains a connec-tion with human reality as *finite*.

I highlight passages from Winnicott's writing (those in italics being central to the case I am making) alongside the poem by Donne. In quoting from each, I juxtapose two distinct forms of writing—the psychological and the poetic—but the phenomena addressed in each are a continuum to be read in sequence and understood as a complementary whole. Infant phenomena, with their reference forward in time, followed by adult phenomena, with their reference backward in time, present the two kinds of

Eros which constitute my "data", much as the quotations from a clinical setting serve as the basis of the argument in clinical papers. I discuss each author, Winnicott and Donne, and their interconnections, representing each as capable of movement forward and backward in time in their understanding of the psyche. By juxtaposing them on the page, I aim for the nearest to simultaneity linear narrative allows, and this formal presentation is inherent to my account.

Winnicott and Donne

Winnicott on infantile attachment, possession, and use of reality in "Transitional Objects and Transitional Phenomena" (1971g)

I.   ORIGINAL HYPOTHESIS

It is well known that infants as soon as they are born tend to use fist, *fingers, thumbs in stimulation of the oral erotogenic zone, in satisfaction of the instincts at that zone, and also in quiet union.* It is also well known that after a few months, infants of either sex become fond of playing with dolls, and that most mothers allow their infants *some special object and expect them to become, as it were, addicted to such objects.*

There is a relationship between these two sets of phenomena which are separated by a time interval, and a study of the development from the earlier into the later can be profitable. . . .

It is clear that something is important here other than oral excitement and satisfaction. . . .

1. The nature of the object.
2. The infant's capacity to recognise the object as "not-me".
3. The place of the object—outside, inside, at the border.
4. The infant's capacity to create, think up, devise, originate, produce an object.
5. The initiation of an affectionate type of object-relationship.

I have introduced the terms "transitional objects" and "transitional phenomena" for the designation of the intermediate area of experience, between the thumb and the teddy bear, *between the oral erotism and the true object relationship*, between primary creative activity and projection of all that has been introjected, *between primary unawareness of indebtedness and the acknowledgement of indebtedness (say "ta")*. [1971g, pp. 1–2, emphasis added]

Later in the same paper, describing the development of a personal pattern by the infant, Winnicott says,

There is plenty of reference in psychoanalytic literature to the progress from "hand to mouth" to "hand to genital", but perhaps less to further progress to the handling of truly "not me" objects. Sooner or later in an infant's development *there comes a tendency on the part of the infant to weave other-than-me objects into the personal pattern.* [p. 3, emphasis added]

Finally, after tracing the touching and mouthing and plucking of soft material or substances, and the accompanying sounds, musical notes, all of which are designated transitional phenomena used by girl and boy alike, used in defensive ways to counter anxiety and depressive ways to address loss, and giving to this area the term "the not-me" possession, present in overt or hidden form, Winnicott states the following:

Summary of Special Qualities in the Relationship
1. The infant assumes rights over the object, and we agree to this assumption. Nevertheless some abrogation of omnipotence is a feature from the start.
2. The object is affectionately cuddled as well as excitedly loved and mutilated.
3. It must never change, unless changed by the infant.
4. It must survive instinctual loving, and also hating and, if it be a feature, pure aggression.
5. Yet it must seem to the infant to give warmth, or to move, or to have texture, or to do something that seems to show it has a vitality or reality of its own.
6. It comes from without from our point of view, but not so from the point of view of the baby. Neither does it come from within; it is not a hallucination.
7. Its fate is to be gradually allowed to be decathected, so that in the course of years it becomes not so much forgotten as relegated to limbo. By this I mean that in health the transitional object does not "go inside" nor does the feeling about it necessarily undergo repression.

It is not forgotten and it is not mourned. It loses meaning, and this is because the transitional phenomena have become diffused, have become spread out over the whole intermediate territory between "inner psychic reality" and "the external world as perceived by two persons in common", that is to say, over the whole cultural field. [1971g, p. 5, emphasis added]

John Donne's "The Good-Morrow": the acknowledgement of adult Eros, intercourse with, and generation of, reality

The Good-Morrow

I wonder by my troth, what thou, and I
Did, till we lov'd? were we not wean'd till then?
But suck'd on countrey pleasures, childishly?
Or snorted we I' the seaven sleepers den?
'T was so; But this, all pleasures fancies bee.
If ever any beauty I did see,
Which I desir'd, and got, 'twas but a dreame of thee.

And now good morrow to our waking soules,
Which watch not one another out of feare;
For love, all love of other sights controules,
And makes one little roome, an everywhere.
Let sea-discoverers to new worlds have gone,
Let Maps to other, worlds on worlds have showne,
Let us possesse our world, each hath one, and is one.

My face in thine eye, thine in mine appeares,
And true plaine hearts doe in the faces rest;
Where can we finde two better hemispheares
Without sharpe North, without declining West?
What ever dyes, was not mixt equally;
If our two loves be one, or, thou and I
Love so alike, that none doe slacken, none can die.

By juxtaposing Winnicott's observations from a study of infants and their reality, based on the psychoanalytic model, which privileges the ascendancy of the analysis of unconscious process in human mentality, with Donne's poem with its assertion that language can intuit meanings in new form, I want to suggest that the term "reality" is appropriate for both contributions. I use the term "reality" to describe that which is *between* what we wish and what we cannot have, and I propose that this is the only place that may be termed "existence". This place presumes creativity, or generation as *necessary*, rather than optional. We have to "realize" only what is possible and to give up what we cannot have in order to make that possible. In this sense, loss creates or generates the real or possible, once what we wish, and what we cannot have, are linked and are recognized as such. Both the psychoanalyst and the poet presume a *need to create, to generate the necessary meaning,* the new form of expression, to give existence to what is desired, as insight or understanding for the analyst observing the infant, as an expression of love between two lovers, and between the poet and the poem for the poet. But this creation, or generation, can only exist within the context of what remains in the internal or desired form, in what *cannot be fully realized,* or, *in all that is also lost in the attribution of externalized meaning.* Generation of meaning sets aside other internal meanings for that moment in real or external time, as it also sets aside the internal meaning in its original form. Thus it gives us, in reality, an apprehension or intuition of truth, defined, concluded for the time being, in this external form. All that is of gain and of loss *is thus simultaneous, cotemporaneous* with the creative or generative act, all gain being intrinsic to loss, and all loss generative of gain.

I now explore four areas of developmental change, from infantile transitional phenomena to adult sexual intercourse, each of which elaborates this in distinct ways.

I

The features of adult Eros that are embedded in, derive from, and refer to (while being fundamentally different from) the features of infantile instinctual attachment *presume, accept, and create in the face of loss.*

> I wonder, by my troth, what thou and I
> *Did,* till we lov'd? were we not wean'd till then?
> But suck'd on countrey pleasures, childishly?

The poet knows, with loving irony, that all that was "done", in the childish past, was mere suckling at the breast and is as nothing to now, as nothing to the adult pleasure of love; "all that" (in infancy) *was done and is over, even though it meant so much—all, in fact, at that time.*

To the Winnicottian infant, whose curiosity and arousal of instincts moves its fingers and thumbs in stimulation of the oral erotogenic zone, there can, initially, be no clear sense of loss; the urgency that is a measure of the adult desire to consummate is not present until repeated loss of the breast creates the need to attach to something external, which leads to the beginning of "playing with dolls", or the move towards the special object to which the infant can become addicted.

Mature genital sex as features of adult Eros recreates this developmental process; the stimulation of the loved object with hands and lips is now extended to full use of all the parts of the body in relation to the loved one (as if, again, an infant in relation to mother's breast and body) in a similar addictive way throughout, and dominantly so in foreplay, or the beginning stages of intercourse. The loved body, in parts, and as a whole, represents the original transitional object as it was and in the initial stages of being used, preparatory for the next and more mature stage of full intercourse. We could call this, getting to know or discovering the object in a possessive way, stimulating the creation of life in the other, through arousal, while unaware, in full, of the presence of that other life and its needs. The infant with the doll—its transitional object—cannot fully differentiate the doll/object from the real, loved, and needed mother as can the adult in the foreplay that leads to full adult intercourse.

From the adult perspective, the poet looks back, as the infant cannot, and comments on infantile desire and pleasure, asking, smilingly ironic in tone, "what did we do then?" a delightful ambiguity that compresses into adult love that we *did* all that ever we could do as infants, but now adult love renders the infantile almost as nothing in comparison. To "do" is also "to have sex", thus tightening the hold of infantile and adult in connection to each other. "What did we do? What kind of erotic play/sex was that when we were babies?" are the questions that Winnicott implies an awareness of in his recognition of something very important to the infant in his relationship to another in these early moments of exploration. Winnicott observes and identifies the addictive, fixated, stimulated, cuddling that is early, rudimentary Eros and validates it as the beginnings of the love that ultimately will lead to engagement with, and love of, all manifestations of reality. The intensity of the infantile, as far as it may go, and the recognition of the vital nature of the transitional object that will be subsumed into adult erotic fulfilment, is the recognition of the adult in the infant, and the infant in the adult.

There is an important distinction, at this stage, between the rudimentary nature of loss for the infant as compared with the recognition, by the adult, of the scale and size of that experience of loss within a growing and developing reality. In a prototypical way, the infant fights to keep his loved connections much as the adult fights to retain the loved one, but the infant's powers to create and generate, compared with those of adults, may be thought of as commensurate with the parallel levels of loss. You cannot know how much you need to create and generate until you have begun to know the size of what you can, and *do*, lose. The well-cared-for infant, hopefully protected from too great a loss, will only develop such creativity as is needed.

Here I am suggesting that healthy and fulfilling adult sexual intercourse is dependent *on the full valuing of what has been lost*, and what therefore needs to be fully generated in new form. Adults who remain restricted in their capacity to acknowledge that desire depends on loss may be unable to mourn in full, and thus they may not wholly regain their erotic life with a fully loved other. The infant who does not or cannot move forward expansively from the breast to the thumb to the teddy to the widening creative circle of play, but repeats and withdraws to one small area, would indicate such a failure to recognize loss and thus be unable to move on to generate.

II

The features of adult Eros that are embedded in, derive from, and refer to (while being fundamentally different from) the features of infantile instinctual attachment *assume the existence of "the other-*

than-me" object, derived from, but also different from and opposed to, the "not-me" self.

'T was so; But this, all pleasures fancies bee.
If ever any beauty I did see,
Which I desir'd, and got, 'twas but a dreame of thee.

The poet knows that what was enjoyed in childhood was different from now and conclusively decides that the past "was so", a version of love (infancy)—certainly not the real thing, because he supposes that all pleasure, all that we take to be pleasurable, by the very nature of the growth that takes us from infancy into adulthood and moves us on, is but a passing "fancy" or fleeting "image", a "phantasy". This is something the poet *can* say in the present, looking back on the past, though at the time the pleasure might have seemed inestimable, as all fancies or illusions do seem when present. Donne distinguishes fancy, illusion, the wish-fulfilling and wish-creating instincts, from the next phase, evident in the last two memorable lines of this stanza.

To return to Winnicott and his five points relating to "The First Possession": he refers to the phase of oral excitement, attachment to, fixation on, and addiction to a special object/toy by the infant. He suggests that the infant *during a time interval* that includes real time—with change, separation, loss intervening—and inner, wish-fulfilling, instinctual time—where having, possessing, attaching, and enjoying timelessly occur—may become aware of the nature of an object, may be able to recognize it as *"not me"*, may position it inside/outside/at the border, in contradistinction and contemporaneously, and may believe in its illusory existence as something created, devised, and produced by the infant and feel affection towards it, not just intense need. Winnicott supposes all this to be the healthy movement from the awareness of the existence of things that are *"not"* the self to something profoundly different which is those things that are *"other"* than the self and are a gift bestowed. "Other" than the self assumes the self to have no part in the creation. "Not" the self still puts the self as central but negated, set aside. It assumes that all that is loved should be as "like the self", as narcissistically "the self", as possible. Such possessive desire places the self very much centre stage. What may appear to be a quibble of a distinction is what separates the infantile, or narcissistic, from the adult, or the object related in the area of love. It is this that the poet beautifully elaborates, through his recognition of all that he cannot create—that is, the loved one and what she brings to him.

In the infant stage the distinction is immaterial: "Did I think this up, produce it, derive it, wish it, conceive it, create it?" To the infant the question—let alone the answer—is, as yet, irrelevant, as it is also to the patient in the early stages of psychoanalysis. To the adult it is vital that he can answer, "I did not: it is other than my creation, I cannot make it, and, thus, I am at the mercy of its loss, with consequences." Thus, "It deserves care, love, protection, preservation against loss by the acts of the self in relation to it. It is outside the remit of the self". However, this loved object is affected by adult sexual generation of intimacy, which creates care, protection, and love. Because the self therefore has a place in relation to the other, a dependence upon it, a gratitude to it, a continuing creative process can unfold.

In the last two lines of the first stanza, Donne's poem subsumes all this into a few words taking us from illusion or fancy, to dream, a profound change of psychic growth, and to an "I" and "You" position, full intercourse. In the final line of that stanza, "If ever any beauty I *did see* . . .", Donne refers to the recognition of *past* pleasure, illusion, enjoyment, *past* "seeing", the state of "looking at" while not yet "possessing". He takes us on, as the infant must go on, from phantasy, which is looking without responsibility, daydreaming, playing in the mind with all that is pleasurable, to actual desiring and getting, "twas but a dream of thee" suggesting that all that was dreamed has brought him to the real "thee", the attainment of the *actual* loved object. The daydreamer who sustains his phantasies over and above reality would not connect his dreaming with the loved one, instead continuing to find fault with reality and keeping his dreams separate and sacrosanct.

Here, Donne's linkage of these two areas—the dreamed and the real—is the recognition of reality derived out of phantasy. These are poetic conceits and plays with language and with love, and they move us because there is a recognition of the process of development. Past dreaming moves forward into reality step by step, the one a preparation for the other. The stages of possession of

and attachment to reality that the Winnicottian infant engages in—
seeking, holding, attributing meaning to the loved object as a real
entity—are, we could say, the provenance of these words and their
meaning. What Donne calls the appropriation, the getting that
follows the desire, a dream of the loved one, are the five points that
Winnicott sees as necessary to the self fully engaging with an
object.

Here, as depicted in the poem, adult Eros prevails over the
rudimentary infantile transitional-object stage by the significant
discrimination or difference between dreaming and illusion, between something that matters not a bit if it is the self or the other,
to something that *must be generated through desire and getting*, which
is a dream of the loved other, who can now become "You". We
have moved from the vague to the definitive, which is the effort
implied by the ability to create dreams and to allow the unconscious room *to make things* that can be wakened from and put to use
in the real world.

Donne's understanding in the poem, that he has always been
"dreaming of the loved one", internally, unconsciously preparing
for the lover, and that, here, and now, finally, she *is* real, *is separate*
to him, and to his dreams, and to his childhood past, all of which
played their part up to this point, means that he can now possess
and enjoy the lover in full, and as an independent being. By this we
move from the "I" of the poem to the "Us", achieving adult intercourse, a union of self and other (not "self" and "not me"), a
consummation and a possible outcome. By contrast, masturbation
phantasies only take place in "I", in *one* mind and body, and can
only generate more of the same, no new "other-than" experience.

The infantile uses of the body—the thumb, the genital area by
itself, and the tendency so to continue—is here distinguished by
the new phase, which Winnicott defines as the handling of truly
"not-me" objects and the weaving of "other-than-me objects into
the personal pattern".

Donne represents this through his poetic achievement and understanding. Both accounts hinge on a vital distinction, the differentiation of "other-than-me" reality from "not-me" reality, a
distinction that has serious consequences in sexual engagement
and fulfilment in reality. The capacity to attach to and love all that

which is quite "other" than the self, even dissonant and at odds with it, is a capacity to engage with the fullness of reality that, as we come steadily to discover, is made up of very little that is us, or our desires, but is far greater, and far less knowable or attainable. To achieve this stage, and not remain at the "this is not me— therefore I reject it" stage, is to grow in real time and, ultimately, develop to the fulfilment that is death.

III

The features of adult Eros that are embedded in, derive from, and refer to, while being fundamentally different from, the features of infantile instinctual attachment *presume a distinction between "that which is no longer" and that which is "vital and continuously alive"*— that is, that Death and Life, though they can be made similar through phantasy, are in reality *different*. This knowledge can then be put to infinite and varied use.

The Winnicottian infant makes powerful attempts to attack, mutilate, and excitedly love/hate the transitional object whose features enable it to survive and maintain a reality of its own despite this kind of attachment. But the infant cannot moderate such instinctual loving and hating towards the object until it becomes aware that the object possesses the characteristics of real life and, consequently, real death. While the infant constructs the transitional object or toy "as real", it is of no consequence how dirty, damaged, or broken it becomes, though it must "survive". Something important must "go on being", even in the toy. Gradually the attachment to real objects that can suffer pain and damage occurs. For instance, the mother who is hurt and cries out in pain when actually attacked by the infant, and who causes the infant distress, ultimately shows herself to be mortal, not indestructible, and attachment to her *in this new way* takes over from the transitional object. This is the decathexis of the transitional object left in a forgotten corner, because now "the real" has taken over from "the toy". For the infant this is the true beginning of a relationship to and use of mortal or finite reality.

In the adult erotic relationship, vital aggressive love/hate, the cuddling which is aggressive-transgressive, the affectionate mutilation of the body (in perverse erotic relations the latter dominant to the point of unrestrained sadism) as part of the testing of the reality of the object that can really suffer if matters go too far, is essential for the acceptance of the life–death borders of a real human being in relation to another. These subtleties of almost going too far, or not going far enough, in erotic play have to be recognized by the lovers and then contribute to full and satisfying intercourse. They are essential to discovering that the body is more than a toy, more than a constantly replaceable phantasy, that the body is capable of living and continuing to live, and therefore capable of death and dying. Going beyond an infantile distinction is essential to adult exploration of the self and other, up to a limited safe point. Just as the transitional object must be kept alive and loved, so with the body of the loved other. (Extreme or unrestrained cruelty in relation to the other—torture, murder, unspeakable sexual perversion—also occupy a place in this spectrum, but in these cases life and death distinctions barely operate.)

All the features that Winnicott describes in the infant's relation to its transitional object apply in the adult erotic relationship. In the infant, these include rights over the loved one, yet abrogation of omnipotence, cuddling, mutilation, the loved one unchanging except at the infant's command, the loved one's survival of the full loving and hating instincts, its ability to express a life of its own, its assuming a place that is neither self-created nor fully the creation of the infant. In the adult, such features must be present in full, with an additional, distinct feature: in the adult erotic relationship, the adult will have come to know what gives and takes life. On the basis of such knowledge, the adult in love may go as far in the full exploration of life as is permitted by such knowledge, while stopping short of the point we call death. A knowledge of the meaning of life and death, unavailable to the infant except in rudimentary form, marks the adult sexual relationship.

The poet, in creating both a portrait of love or of lovers in love in his poem, and creating the poem itself (a "still-life form of love") generates, as does the creative couple in intercourse, an outcome, a new form of life, the never-before poem. This the infant cannot do.

Although it has the illusion that it can, the infant cannot create the thumb, the blanket, the teddy, all these initially deriving loving meaning from the life-giving breast of the mother. The lovers, moving beyond illusion, can generate the sperm, the egg, the fertilizing process, and eventually the infant, just as the poet can create the completed poem. In the adult and the poetic coupling, the reality of procreation and creation is accepted and used in full. The creation of full intercourse, experienced and known in full, like the creation of the completed poem, is a contribution to and an augmentation of the real: the real infant or the real poem may each be seen as defining of reality; they are products that cannot be contested or relegated to illusion. We might say that illusion is a stage of the real, and many stop short, there, but the more we do/ create (the Greek word for poem means a "doing" or "making", a poem as a thing made or created) the more we "realize" and "make real".

Through the relationship to the transitional object, the infant is enabled potentially to create meaningful connections that again represent the procreative or fertile process in its prototypical form. And in not being able to do what the adults can do generatively, it is indebted to the parental couple, much in the way that the non-creative among us are indebted to the procreative artists, scientists, and all contributors to culture or generation.

The poet who knows that human love is transient does not stop at the enjoyment of human love—that short-term illusion that only lasts a life—but, rather, goes on to create the undying verse that houses such transience, permanently, for all to enjoy. This is what I referred to earlier as the necessity to create through the awareness of loss. The poem is the writer's artefact of love, an embodiment of the experience of love in a shape and form that is utterly new, created solely from, and out of, that intercourse. Intercourse here refers not only to the experience of love, but to a lasting encounter between the poet and his poem as they come together into words. The young infant embarks upon a similar "making and doing" when he draws shapes, sings snatches of music, creates sounds and meanings in language, all from an intercourse with life as a whole, derived from the loved parents, who are the initial reality, a reality from which he produces his own new creations. The work of concentration that ultimately produces the poem assumes just such an intercourse, but one that is far more sophisticated and worked for than the infant's, one that has access to tools that expand the repertoire of possibilities, just as infinite sexual exploration and experimentation develops adult sexuality. The child, the poet, the lover each experiments and seeks to expand the range of expression, as do the development of transitional objects and phenomena into the wider cultural field. The growing and enjoying that takes the child into adulthood is paralleled for the poet and the lover who will want to "do" or create more and more from increasing pleasurable experience and experimentation.

In Donne's final two stanzas the symbol of the child awakening from infant illusions into living out his dream of love, in full daylight, into the having of love's dream in the reality of day, is achieved. We can admire the movement into *symbolic* life, the intricate imagery that compares love to the discovery of new worlds that range no further than the faces and eyes of the loved ones who gaze at each other. Such imagery emphasizes the fictional nature of love in the time that life offers, not for ever, but in the breadth and expanse of a poem and its wide-ranging allusions. The emphasis on the future is contained in the "good-morrow", the promise of infinite day, the beginning to enjoy its offers of union in the small world of the bedroom, the movement all the while between waking up to something and yet remaining dream-like somewhere asleep, permanently transfixed in love, in possession of one another, timelessly, as in dreams or poems. And all this the poet must energetically "love/hate" into the real words that he must find, destroying the words of others, the clichés, the earlier poems, so that this poem survives/lives. All that is difficult beyond words, all that is surprising in the revelation of words, all that is life and death giving from each must be passed through, in real time, for the poem to form and finally exist, alone on the page.

The poem is a creation from and by the poet in relation to his inner world, with all the skills he can bring to bear on it, but it is not a phantasy or an illusion; it is there on the page, unlike the dream. *It is realized.* This is also the progress to full genital intercourse that reaches climax and fulfilment in a sexual coupling producing infants or other manifestations of creativity in real terms. Stopping short of such full and complete consummation will not "do". Or perhaps one could say, failure and frustration here is all too familiar, the infantile "play" at sex, intruding on the adult consummation of sex. A good poem on the page, if fully responded to, does not play with and then finally cheat the reader; rather, it delights to its final consummating lines:

> What ever dyes was not mix't equally;
> If our two loves be one, or, thou and I
> Love so alike, that none doe slacken, none can die.

Here there is what no infant can appreciate, and it is done with the full playfulness and skill of an adept adult, the poet and lover, who has worked his way up, in time, all the way from infancy. The protestation to the loved one, albeit and by necessity playfully, punning in words (because reality is between what we wish and what we cannot have, and words are the best we can have, for the poet, at least, since real life passes eventually), is that love, which is life, must be sustained by both lovers in equal measure, just as, to get a proper dye, or mix, of two substances, equal measures must be given. All this, of course, is a living sensual and sexual image. And so we have "none doe slacken", each lover giving equally to the other, the pun on dying, mixing dyes/colours equally referring to death—in the attempt to secure life, *and if, if, if* all this can stream forth, this sexual life from one and the other, and from one *to* the other, the poet suggests there will be no loss, a pretty conceit, indeed! This way, he suggests, we cannot lose—instead death is defeated! Should this turn out not to be quite true, the poet creates the poem, which, in its beautiful equilibrium of attributes, creates a perpetuity of "seeming-life" in living form. The poet does not take the risk of leaving life to its devices. He knows life will fade, the colours of love will gradually wear, but the poem remains and will do office instead. The poet's serious addiction to poetry making, like the infant's to his transitional object, establishes this without question. The poem is not the same as the love or the lovers, nor the love and the lovers the same as the poem. The awareness of difference is repeatedly acknowledged in art. Knowing that love dies, the poet "dyes", or mixes his love with his love of words to produce the fast colours of verse.

IV

The feature of adult Eros that is embedded in, derived from, and refers to (while being fundamentally different from) the features of infantile instinctual attachment is *the capacity for the sublime in all its features, which originally was, for the infant, the experience of joy, now so transformed in the adult as to require new language to meet new meaning.*

Once the infant has moved on from the transitional object towards the whole cultural field, the transitional object decathected and relegated to limbo, the infant's potential relationship to, and use of, reality is described by Winnicott in the following significant words:

> the transitional *object does not "go inside" nor does the feeling about it necessarily undergo repression. It is not forgotten and it is not mourned.* It loses meaning, and this is because the transitional phenomena have become diffused, have become spread out over the whole intermediate territory between "inner psychical reality" and "the external world as perceived by two persons in common". [1971g, p. 5, emphasis added]

In this description of the gradual spread of meaning from the original transitional object into the wider sphere, I want to explore a difference from infantile to adult and the potential for a full sublimation of the instincts expressed in one form through adult genitality. We might say that, although the transitional object is relegated to limbo, loses meaning, and remains unmourned, nevertheless all its features, as described earlier by Winnicott, are found and invested *in new form* as the adult loved object. This would constitute one sense in which transitional phenomena extend over the whole intermediate territory between "inner psychic reality" and "the external world as perceived by two persons in common".

However, I want to suggest that there is something about the adult state of consummation, sometimes described as the fearful ecstasy created in union, that may be distinguished from what Winnicott defines as "excitement" in the infant and may be said to approach the state of the sublime. This would be a possible, but not inevitable, feature of full adult sexuality but is never possible in infant experience. There are connections between infantile and adult experience, but there are also differences—differences that are substantially and profoundly different from the existence of the infantile within adult experience.

In the area of what I am calling the potential for the occurrence of the sublime (and I would include in here the sublime as terror and awe in the face of the infinite and all unknowing), in the consummation between two adults in mature genital sexuality, we might, with the support of art and culture, posit the following. The sublime—defined as "of ideas, truths, subjects etc; Belonging to the highest regions of thought, reality or human activity" (*O.E.D.*)—is both part of thought, part of reality, and part of human activity, all of which, at any one moment, may be gathered up into one meaning which is human sexual intercourse at its height. It can also be the revelation of the divine in all the products of human culture. But it is in the area of the sublime that *the need for the full, not partial, abrogation of omnipotence* (to refer back to the Winnicottian infantile self) is made by the human self, whether alone or in union. The loss of the centrality of self, the subsuming of the self to all that is present in creation prior to human presence or intervention coming from "we know not where", allows us also to invest the loved object who, as part of the unknown creation, is felt to be beyond all understanding. This raises the level of the human to the level of mystery and transfiguration. The capacity for this elevation or transfiguration is only possible if the loved one is recognized, *symbolically*, as representative of all that is "Creation". This means that *the loved one is part of the whole, and that this whole or Creation in all its features is of monumental scale and design, therefore above and beyond, as well as outside, our human remit*. The recognition of the proportions here of part to whole, and the size and scale of creation, would be part of the movement towards all that elicits awe, the divine, the infinite, the sublime. For an experience of this, even in fragmentary form, in the greatest aesthetic works of civilization, or in glimpses, in the mystery of human intercourse, there would have to be a total absence of that "knowing self" commonly held as highly prized. For most of us, this relinquishing of knowing is scarcely within the bounds of possibility, since the striving for a knowing mastery is part of the will to life. In this area, the will to life is contested by the will to death—that is, the movement unequivocally in the direction that moves away from life, as much as towards, and within it.

In the infant, the features of "excitement" (Winnicott's word)—
and, one would say, increasingly, the capacity for joy—have to be
transformed by the adult into the new form and new meaning that
has the attributes of the sublime. The difference here lies not just in
abrogation of the omnipotence of self, but equally in the elevation
of all that is loved and "other than self". For the infant, the thumb
or blanket or teddy is not "higher than". For the adult in true
fulfilment, the object created, whether loved object, work of art, or
manifestation of the sublime in some other form, must be felt to be
profoundly "greater than" the ordinary "I" or "You" of reality; it
forms part of imagined or visionary reality rather than what "is".
The features of pleasure of the infantile can never compete with the
recognition of the self here defined as abiding below the heights of
the sublime and, at moments, achieving transcendent experience.

In Donne's magisterial sweep of reference, in his likening of the
lovers to all beauty ever seen, desired and got, and his acknowledgement of it as but a dream of the loved one, he brings the
infinite into human compass, suggests human love as one part of
the sublime, proves it in his argument for the new and transcendent worlds waiting beyond him for discovery, and likens this
mysterious journey to the journey of intercourse in the heights of
love. These images are the so-called metaphysical traits of this
writing; it is such imaginings, such form here achieved in one small
poem, that speaks eloquently of what we long to know. Donne's
great sermons, which follow his poetic writings, are perhaps expressions of the concentration upon human Eros giving way to,
and moving on, to the expression of divine Eros.

Such divine readings of reality are prototypically present in that
which takes the infant forward to accomplish his desire. As he ages
into sexual manhood, it is his retaining of that desire, beyond
human sexuality and in the service of the sublime, that would, in
the face of the increasing losses sustained, secure him within experience as infinite. This is a very different vision from the death
instinct of Freud and Klein, of analysis terminable and intermina-
ble. Such vision remains trapped within the human circuit in its
quest for knowledge and never moves, imaginatively, into the full
acceptance of Freud's original discoveries of the unconscious as
unknowable. "Unknowable" here carries the meaning of "filling one
with awe", since the unconscious is unknowable and unfathomable

and draws us in to the indefinable or the sublime. Winnicott's formulations allow for the development within real time eventually into neither real nor internal time but into that which is the infinite. And here the discourse of poetry and the discourse of psychoanalysis, these interlinked disciplines, may become difficult to distinguish in the attempt to approach and define that which is unknowable; the terrain challenges both discourses and their limitations, leading to a language that may appear to be poor poetry and poor psychoanalysis. Consummation here is with all that is beyond the human, preparing the way for the return to matter or "dust" that all of us eventually become; the discourse here is wordless.

Conclusion

The four areas of developmental change from infantile transitional phenomena to adult sexual intercourse, the latter with its links to the earlier attempts to express desire, possession, and the uses of reality, are my own derivatives from the writings of Winnicott as they may be understood in relation to a work of art that speaks of Eros. We move from the infantile possession and use of reality to intercourse with, and generation of transcendent, reality as the infantile moves into the adult, old age, and death.

This study makes no definitive claim for the features of adult sexuality and its achievement, and, indeed, quite other features of the texts of Winnicott and of the Donne text could have been drawn upon. But in the connections and differences discussed here, I have tried to delineate the early erotic and sexual form of transitional objects and phenomena, and their transformations in later life, and to offer an account of what may be the abiding nature of these features while charting the steps that time brings. It is the awareness of time that allows for monumental alterations in the adult sexual psyche, distinguishing it fundamentally from that of its infantile beginnings. Art and psychoanalysis allow us, in their different ways, to study and approach the discrete features that enable such alterations to proceed, allowing us more scope to define the healthy adult sexual psyche in its confrontations with the passage of real rather than infantile or phantasy time.

Note

For the reader who wishes to be directed to Winnicott's concerns and formulations on sexuality along the lines of this chapter, I would suggest a study of Chapter One, Part Two, "Interpersonal Relations", of his late text, *Human Nature* (1988). The rest of the book is more generally supportive of this view.

CHAPTER SEVEN

Sex as a defence against sexuality

Mario Bertolini & Francesca Neri

In front the slender man in the blue mantle,
Gazing in dumb impatience straight before him.
His steps devoured the way in mighty chunks
They did not pause to chew; his hands were hanging,
Heavy and clenched, out of the falling folds,
No longer conscious of the lightsome lyre,
The lyre which had grown into his left
Like twines of rose into a branch of olives.
It seemed as though his senses were divided:
For, while his sight ran like a dog before him,
Turned round, came back, and stood, time and time again,
Distant and waiting at the path's next turn,
His hearing lagged behind him like a smell.

Rilke, *Orpheus, Eurydice, Hermes* (1964, p. 143)

Rilke seems here to be describing two separate registers used by man in his attempt to understand and relate to reality. One of the two, motility, predominantly sensory, is directed towards external reality: with this, Orpheus "devours" the path. The other, predominantly perceptual, has to do with internal reality; it is through this register that he perceives Eurydice as the echo inside himself, even though her footsteps are silent.

If only he had been able to imagine Eurydice through his hearing, Orpheus might have had his "beloved" back. Instead, he was overwhelmed by the desire to look towards the echo, in the same way as his steps "devoured the way in mighty chunks,/ they did not pause to chew" (p. 143).

For the poet, the echo that comes from internal reality—the one behind, that cannot be seen—is the impetus that quickens Orpheus's step, and the urgency of his footsteps confirms its importance. The echo represents *feelings* of union; the urgency represents separation *anxieties.*

Rilke is suggesting, perhaps, that Orpheus cannot bear the fact of union without separation, and vice versa, and so he imagines these two aspects of himself as if they were one, as equivalents. In looking back, Orpheus is denying that what he feels inside himself, an internal echo, can only be imagined, not seen. Hermes is inflexible in demanding from Orpheus the proof that the purely somatic components of the instinctual life and the symbolic experience are not separate or alternative states.

What we want to develop here is that this kind of split is at the root of significant disturbances in the sexuality of certain individuals, in whom sexuality may find itself—precisely as the poet imagines Orpheus—unsatisfied by the purely bodily aspects of sex.

Orpheus reflects the precipices and turning points in the path through changes in his vision, as his eye runs back and forth. This sensorimotor skill is capable of insisting on the pretence of objectivity: intent on devouring the path with his eyes and his footsteps, Orpheus is rewarded by a primarily muscular demonstration that he exists in relation to the path.

On the other hand, this does not account for his entire experience. The perception of an echo that comes from inside disturbs his ability to make reality equivalent to bodily modifications; it enables him to perceive a reality different from the first, one that has nothing to do with bodily sensations (Eurydice's footsteps make no noise). There is a moment when the echo appears to pose an unwanted question, one that is impossible to answer: responding with action to the desire for union means losing the echo of the absence of the object, and this results in its disappearance. The symbol of Orpheus's being in love cannot be accessed either by his sensations or by his actions, it is not accompanied by any bodily changes, and it cannot be reduced to bodily sensation.

If the sensory register has to do with the need to exist in relation to the path, then the register of perception has to do with the desire to feel real, to exist in relation to oneself. There should be a place where Orpheus feels that his conflicting experiences can co-exist— both the experience of searching for union with Eurydice in his urgency to reach her physically, and the experience of feeling separated from her, because he is connected to her only symbolically. If this place does not exist, then he has to free himself from ambiguity to avoid the fear of going mad. He does it by turning around and looking at her, using the only tool at his disposal: his sense of sight. It is interesting that in this myth, tragedy (Eurydice's disappearance) coincides with the unsustainability of the conflict between the two facets of Orpheus himself. "The tragic is a collision, a thing in between, an amphibious area between two others. The tragic happens if one of the two parties to the collision wins out, destroying the other" (Kierkegaard, 1843).

It was Winnicott (1971b) who described the function of an intermediate state between union and separation, between subject and object. A child can feel that there could be an area or a state between "me" and "not me" that is filled in play by the symbols of union. Winnicott writes: "The use of an object symbolizes the union of two now separate things, baby and mother, *at the point in time and space of the initiation of their state of separateness*" (pp. 96–97).

There is no equivalence between sex and sexuality, just as there is no equivalence between internal/external space and potential space. But sex, in its instinctual manifestation, can sometimes function as a defence against sexuality, in the same way that Orpheus's retreat to the sensory functioned as a defence against a pyschophysical relationship with Eurydice.

Intermediate space is brought into existence not only through the work of the subject, but also because the object shares and participates in the pleasure of a pre-logical merger of subject and object (Milner, 1952). In this respect, Rilke gives a detailed description of Eurydice's state as Orpheus is walking in front of her, registering the sound, the perfume, and the internal echo of her footsteps:

But hand in hand now with that god she walked,
Her pace, circumscribed by lengthy shroudings,
uncertain, gentle, and without impatience,
wrapt in herself, like one whose time is near,
she thought not of the man who went before them,
nor of the road ascending into life.
Wrapt in herself she wandered. And her deadness
Was filling her like fullness.
Full as a fruit with sweetness and with darkness
Was she with her great death, which was so new
That for the time she could take nothing in. [p. 145]

Perhaps Orpheus felt the echo of Eurydice as a symbol of what she was for him, but, given what she was expressing in her face, he must have doubted that what he was perceiving represented anything real.

If the myth sees humanity as unable to pay the price of doubt and uncertainty in order to feel real, Rilke here appears to be opening up an area of debate that will be elaborated, above all, by Winnicott. Winnicott proposed that to feel real it is necessary not only for the subject to be aware of his or her own desires, but to recognize the willing participation of the other in his or her play. If this is missing, Eurydice's face does not mirror Orpheus's joy, and Orpheus cannot feel real either in relation to his symbols or in relation to himself. He is forced to seek refuge in doing and the omnipotence of the senses, leaving the state of being split-off.

If what was missing for Orpheus, given Eurydice's depression and her lack of thought for the man walking in front of her, were the intermediate space of experience, intermediate between him and her, might it not then be possible to think of Orpheus as deprived of the presence of someone who is interested in holding and containing him?

Such a way of conceptualizing—highlighted here by reading Rilke's poem in the light of Winnicott—represents a radical difference in its implications for psychoanalytic treatment, and one that has led to significant changes in technique. In the shifts from "classical" psychoanalysis to contemporary practices, it is not only a matter of how our patients have changed (Gaddini, 1984), but also how the analyst has changed. For us, this change can be identified through the ways the patient presents and enacts his or her psychic reality in the sessions, and in the ways he or she makes the analyst aware of it.

Re-reading the myth of Orpheus through the poetry of Rilke, an analyst of the first generation might see the effects of an unsuccessful repression. Orpheus was not capable of experiencing the echo as the representation of his own preconscious desire. In a part of himself, perhaps he had repressed his desire for Eurydice; the disturbance he felt could then be linked to a sudden return of what was repressed (the desire) manifesting itself as the need to possess.

A contemporary analyst would look for other dimensions—for instance, in relation to Orpheus's oscillation between a certainty that reality corresponds to his own sensory responses and doubts about whether reality exists outside his own omnipotence or whether existence is only about sexual orgasm.

From this perspective, a contemporary analyst might be tempted to ask what one of his or her patients saw in the face of the other during sex. The patient might see a female or male slave, ready to satisfy his or her needs; if so, he or she would then be forced to experience the sexual act as a primarily physical one aimed at concrete possession. Or the patient might see an expression of maniacal gaiety that masked the anxiety of penetrating or being penetrated. In this case, the patient would be forced to begin penetration and then run away for fear of being annihilated.

The expressions of what a patient might see in the face of the other during the sexual act become more extended and multifaceted the more experience we have of the transference of the patient in our own countertransference.

In our clinical experience, the deprivation suffered by borderline patients is made concrete even in their sexual relations. In both the analytic transference and their everyday lives, these patients hallucinate in the other what they *feel but do not know* to have been the salient characteristics of their mothers' experience of motherhood. The word "hallucination" seems appropriate here for describing both a way of perceiving the other that is exclusively sense-based and not symbolic, and the characteristic of re-finding in the other not an object separate from the self, but a representation of the merged object.

Clinical case study

A late adolescent (21 years) asks for an analysis, because he does not know how to deal with his sense of his own uselessness about his life.

Despite his youth and average education, he is successful in carrying out an important role in the family business. His whole way of presenting himself, whether in his choice of dress or otherwise, imitates a City broker, and he seems to pride himself on showing off a black briefcase. In the (male) analyst's countertransference, this briefcase is the phallic extension of himself. The patient actually states that he never puts anything important or essential in the case. It does, however, provide a cunning device to enable him to have his analysis with me, to present himself to me, and to imagine that he is being regarded by me with respect, but also with suspicion. Thanks to the black bag—empty, but with the capacity to make a visual impact upon me—he feels he is identical to me and I am identical to him. He sees me as a successful man, because from the beginning I have appeared competent, and a bit abrupt—in other words, a successful man, just like him.

After several months, he tells me that he does not have any sexual problems with girls, that he has had an active and intense sex life since the age of 17, that he is very selective and particular in his choice, and that he certainly does not run away from sex. But he has not had a stable relationship yet, because that would tire him out. It irritates him—he doesn't know why—to be in the same room as a woman with whom he has just had sex. He *goes away* immediately after. He then describes how he escapes by taking a long, fast walk, or running until his legs get tired; only then does he stop.

While he tells me these things, he makes me feel that I am with him in the intertwining of various opposing feelings. It is as if a kind of over-investment in physical energy might fetishistically console him precisely for his lack of aliveness and for the feeling of being weak and useless that is both connected to, and in conflict with, his excessive sexual activity.

Perhaps, like Orpheus, this patient wanted to run away from a libidinal obstruction. His need to love and feel loved is not satisfied by his attempts to discharge it by going through the motions of having sex; it continues to choke his ego, so his next attempt to defend himself from the situation of danger is to get rid of his anxiety by running away.

It is worth noting that he is the younger of two siblings. The other brother is fifteen years his senior and is like his father, from whom he inherited the technical side of operations in the business when the father died of cancer.

The patient was born after another child had died at the age of 3 years, and he was given the same name. In his "family romance", he, by his birth, had saved his mother from depression. As soon as he was born, he was sent away and brought up by two unmarried paternal aunts. He only came back to the family home when he had passed the age at which his brother had died, because it would not have been right "for my mother to bring up another child for nothing".

The patient's inability to feel any aggression towards his mother was remarkable. And in the transference he communicated a malleability in submitting himself to me, as if he were submitting to a successful competent man, who is without interest in him. Through this meekness in the here-and-now, he re-lived the way he had submitted to his depressed mother.

He made me feel that even sexual relations had the advantage of submission. Through his flights, he sought the advantage of denial, discharging in the activity of his muscles the hate he felt for the women to whom, through his seduction of them, he was in reality submitting himself, through his compulsion to re-live his primitive primary relationships.

Perhaps, again like Orpheus, he had to run away, to escape into activity. In his case he was running from his mother, in whose face he must have seen, alongside gentleness, a lack of interest in the child in front of her.

Perhaps, in coming to analysis to be me, he was exhibiting the phallus by displaying the bag, so that I, in turn, would imitate him, become phallic, and thereby collude with him in maintaining the advantages of an eternal fusion. The price he paid was his sense of feeling unreal and useless.

For a long time, he made me feel that he was expecting either a scandalized reproach or my collusive protection if he confessed his homosexual relations with a fellow student on his evening course, who was the same age as his elder brother. He submitted himself to him in the same way as he did in his relationships with women: without interest or passion.

In the countertransference, I felt uneasy about being experienced as a man. Moreover, I did not really feel I was one, and I knew that this rebellion came from the sense of my own bodily presence in the sessions. I wondered who that part of him was, that, feeling feminine, directed itself towards me, with the certainty that I would be seduced by it. Sometimes I felt as if the patient was not engaging in a dialogue with me, but carrying on a monologue and, really, was interested in shutting me up. Maybe he felt that the seduction was unreal, or that he was repeating with his analyst the pseudo-relationships he played out through sex. But his main aim seemed to be to avoid a real relationship, and to avoid feeling any conflict with or difference from his analyst.

If submitting to me and seducing me were his counter-phobic tools for avoiding feeling any conflict or difference between him and me in the transference, then it was this that was the real danger for him. His defensive counter-phobic positions seemed to contain the awareness of a danger so terrible that he had learned to pre-empt it. In this way he avoided what, at other times and in other places, he had experienced with such anxiety. Perhaps sex in purely physical terms, at least up to his flight from the person with whom he had just had that sex, was a strikingly noticeable way of discharging his anxiety about difference through his muscles.

It was Schur (1958) who elaborated Freud's *Inhibitions, Symptoms and Anxiety* (1926d [1925]) and described "somatization" as the main defence used to discharge anxiety. He proposed the "desomatization of anxiety" as the journey from avoidance not to a merely somatic awareness of being able to feel small and in need of the help of the other, but to an intrapsychic awareness. In terms of my patient, he could do everything but feel that he was someone's child.

Little Hans could not bear there to be any difference between his own body and that of his mother; differences could only exist between him and inanimate objects such as chairs. Following our account, the peeing of the horse would be the counter-phobic object through which Little Hans discharged, in more socially acceptable terms, his phobia of his mother's bodily and psychological femininity.

This patient, however, did not condense his phobia into an external object (A. Freud, 1967). Instead, he distributed it among his interpersonal and analytic relationships, and, in so doing, he ensured they could not become objects outside his own omnipotence.

I tried to let him know that his anxieties were necessary for him to be what he was, and that all I could do was to acknowledge them. But for him to seem what he was not—for instance, the City broker—he felt he had to have his well-cut grey suits. Through them he felt he would regain the advantage because his anxiety would be wiped out if the areas of difference and conflict between him and me were wiped out. I often had the feeling that interpretations of content were neither necessary nor wanted, that the only way I could support him was to accept the reality of his anxiety.

He dreamt of women who were nude from the waist down, their breasts covered in furs, necklaces, and feathers. When we wondered together about how strange these women seemed, he said that they were not whole women, and his associations were to the garments of the men of primitive peoples, which, by covering the penis, simultaneously allude to it.

I could imagine, and I suggested this interpretation to him, that a masculine woman might engage with him and look at him as a woman. Perhaps it was this that we had not been able to imagine when he had told me at the beginning that he saw me as a man— that is, that he was actually a woman to whom I, as a man, would be attracted. Perhaps this was the ability he spoke of. And, in this way, he would be the breast, with which he could feed me and save me from depression. Something similar had happened between him and his mother, whom effectively he had had to save from the depression of not being able to be a mother either to the dead brother or to him.

I also thought that this was the way he defended himself from his anxiety about the difference between his body and a woman's. Perhaps becoming the breast avoided castration anxiety, and he then looked for confirmation of this by having lots of sex. While necessary to avoid castration anxiety, however, sex was useless for making him feel really himself. His anxiety was therefore not linked with his fear of women, but with his sense of uselessness, and of not existing, the feelings that had initially brought him to analysis.

> In such conditions the ego's central defence is fetishistic: to disavow reality on a specific point, a fracture in the sense of reality. There is one part that knows and defends itself with the counter-investment of neurosis, and a part which does not know, does not want to know, and is engaged in denial. The void in the real left by denial is filled by the unreality of the fetish. [Masciangelo, 1988, p. 27]

It was Freud who spoke of the child's polymorphous experiences and proposed this term "polymorphous", a stroke of genius. Patients who use sex to defend themselves from sexuality have significant problems in the sense of self. Not only the object, but also the image of the self is polymorphous—that is to say, divided into separate, partial, non-integrated images. The image of a half-woman and, correspondingly, of a half-child and a half-man is an iconic illustration of this point.

In "The Split-off Male and Female Elements to be Found in Men and Women" (1966), Winnicott writes: "the pure female element relates to the breast (or to the mother) in the sense of *the baby becoming the breast (or mother), in the sense that the object is the subject.* I can see no instinct drive in this . . . Here in this relatedness of pure female element to 'breast' is a practical application of the idea of the subjective object . . ." (p. 177).

The polymorphous aspects of self-images have overtones of identifications and incorporations with the primary object, above all if one takes into account that the need to incorporate mainly has to do with objects that are bad or rejecting, since the incorporated object cannot then reject (Fairbairn, 1952). Also, the transformation of the bad object into something first outside and conflictual, then external and different, can happen afterwards.

Women's breasts appeared again at a more advanced stage in this analysis, and two dreams were significant at that time. In one, *the patient's analyst is on his way to his house, the much-loved house where he first lived with his parents, after he had been fostered by his aunts. His analyst has a bag in his hand and he is going to the patient's house to make him a meal and is bringing what he needs with him.* Some months later, he dreamed of his mother: *she is young, beautiful, and comes towards him smiling. She is wearing a silk dress, which shows off her curves. She also has a bag for shopping. The patient asks, "Have I never told you that my mother is a good cook?" His mother is crossing the most beautiful square in his town, Santa Maria Formosa.*

In the oedipal scenario to which these dreams belong, there begins to be a place for a man and for nourishment by the mother. There is also a more realistic bodily and psychological image of himself, and the images of women are now whole.

The advent of sexuality and its transformation into a sexed and sexual identity seems to be favoured by the facilitating environment of analysis and, in particular, by the intermediate space between patient and analyst. In this space, the patient can experiment with the fear of feeling lost in the spaces of detachment and separateness, so long as the other person also participates by supporting the echo of him/herself in the subject.

Discussion

1.   A sense of uselessness and futility can be hidden by sexual acts through which the subject attempts defensively to concretize his strength as fetish. The non-integration between somatic—or, in this case, sexual—strength and pyscho-physical aliveness is confined neither to men nor to women, nor to homosexual or heterosexual relationships.

In our experience as psychoanalysts and psychiatrists of adolescents, it is a fairly frequent occurrence, and one of its characteristics is the possibility of remaining asymptomatic for varying lengths of time.

What we have tried to suggest in this chapter is that there has to be a process that takes place between non-integration and integration. Sex and sexuality are not integrated from the start: even in a healthy adolescent, sex exists before sexuality. His or her pregenital experiences in infancy re-emerge as such at the onset of adolescence. In a number of adolescents, fortunately not many, non-integration must be maintained, and the division between aspects of the false self and denigrated aspects of the true self is reinforced defensively. Having sex can function as an acceptable counter-phobic defence, which is sometimes even socially celebrated. Obviously, as in the case described above, this goes hand in hand with other counter-phobic defences that can help avoid the psychic pain that comes from the awareness of a sense of personal identity as distinct and independent from that of the object.

2. Sexual acts, like interpersonal relationships more generally, or the ability to take on new tasks, such as studying, are secretly felt to be both useless and necessary. In the analyst's countertransference, it is as if the adolescent were asking himself, "What will I do with myself, and with my sex?" In borderline cases, the answer might be, "I have to act on it, or I'll be disturbed by the question." Enactment thus becomes a necessity, an obligation, but it is one that is useless for resolving the enigma of the self. A gulf can thus open up, and be maintained, between "me and my self" (Khan, 1979, p. 116).

In the patients of this kind, what cannot be integrated seems not to be the functioning of the sexual organ but, rather, the perception of a sexualized self (Laufer & Laufer, 1989). In the patient whose case is outlined, what had to be avoided was the integration of the physical arena of sex with the psychic one. In this respect, we think sexuality becomes the negative of sex.

> In experience and in psychoanalytic theory sexuality does not only designate the activity and the pleasure that derives from the functioning of the genital apparatus but all the excitations and activities already present in infancy that produce a pleasure that is irreducible to the satisfaction of a basic physiological need and that are found as components of the so called normal forms of sexual love. [Laplanche & Pontalis, 1967, translated for this edition]

Laplanche and Pontalis describe this work of the negative with the term, "irreducible".

In our opinion, the integration of the pleasure obtained from the sexual organ with "everything that cannot be reduced to this" is the ability to feel internally responsible for sexual pleasure as both a psychic and a bodily way of reaching and experiencing being welcomed and held by the object. The private gaps or blanks that these patients re-live in the transference with the secondary object-analyst repeat the obliterations that were necessary in the relationship with the primary object—namely, the pre-oedipal mother. Becoming the breast and seducing the depressed mother so as to save her was this patient's way of not feeling wounded by the trauma of environmental failure.

In a letter to Fliess (21 September 1897), Freud expressed his doubts about the usefulness of seduction theory and the inaccessibility of the motives for which sexuality, above all, was so forcibly repressed. "Even in the most serious psychoses, unconscious memories do not emerge, the secrets of infantile experiences are not revealed even in states of confusion and delirium. Again, even in the most favorable conditions for the exploration of the unconscious none of the initial elements ultimately emerge" (Freud, 1990, p. 117). Perhaps the secrets of infantile experiences refer to the need for seduction as a way of reacting to a traumatic experience without having to feel harmed by it. Only many years later, in *Moses* (1939a [1937–39]), would Freud give a detailed description of traumatic experience as man's capacity and need to feel unharmed by the trauma undergone.

3.   The psychoanalytic literature on trauma is vast, but for us it was Ferenczi (1933) who first approached the central question of the psychodynamics of denial and splitting. He thought that not feeling harmed by trauma was a necessity, which functioned, above all, as the externalized aspect of the inability to suffer for the injury undergone. This depended on the fact that certain adults, because of their own pathology, imposed their own language of passion onto the child, instead of allowing the child's language of tenderness to be listened to and valued by them. The consequence of this would be confusion: the child, not recognized as someone's child, had to adopt the language of passion and of the body—that is, the language of the pathological adult.

Taking a different route, Winnicott identified private lacks and their pathological development in the non-existence of an intermediate space, the only kind of space in which the two different types of language could come together and slowly be integrated.

For his part, Ferenczi indicated the need for trust, "a certain I do not know what", that could make the present experience different from the pathogenic experience of the past. It is interesting that "trust" for Ferenczi and "reliability" for Winnicott relate to the perception of a difference between present and past, but the perception of difference itself has no cognitive reference; it is something lived and experienced without reference to content.

4.   There is a moment when the analyst feels that the patient, in talking about his defences, *is actually putting his life force into the analyst*. The patient feels he is recounting the facts, but there is a discrepancy between the facts recounted and what the patient makes the analyst feel. The analyst feels that there is a particular aspect of the mental functioning of the patient, which is the need to leave his mark on the analyst. Sometimes it is not possible to discern the shape or weight of such a mark: it might seem to have totally unreal aspects, but it is still worth being experienced, registered, and elaborated upon. It could be the need, however confused, to make one's own presence felt, even if by doing so it means inflicting unease on the analyst.

In our experience with borderline patients, this energy, a capacity to exert *a weight on and into the other*, is experienced in the countertransference before the patient's own perception of it. The ability to feel one's own weight, one's own consistency, is initially an intrusion of the subject into the object, which is concretized by taking over the person of the analyst. An exaggerated form of cathexis *can become* a defensive reassurance against the fear of emptiness that comes from the other's indifference. It can also be manifested in fetishistic phenomena, as we have shown above.

The patient's need to leave an imprint on the other (Bertolini, 1999) has to do with both death and life. In the case of death, if the other is destroyed and so cannot contain inside himself the imprint of the subject, then the subject feels he does not exist; in the case of life, if, after having been marked, the object can confirm to the subject that he exists inside himself through the imprint, this becomes the way of communicating something real: "you exist because you make me feel that you do."

It takes time for these communications to be made, transmitted, and perceived by the other and registered in the self. This could be thought of as an intermediate time between not being heard and beginning to be heard. In cases where the analysis continues, it is also the time when the traumatic experiences of the past can be contrasted with the less traumatic experiences of the present.

5.   The growing awareness of the analyst's countertransference helps in directing attention to those aspects in which the patient's vital energies become more intensely invested even though the patient himself feels he has to fight against the loss of both self and object at all costs. In this way, the false self acts to build and reinforce the ability to deny or to keep split-off the anxieties and the sense of danger to which the patient would be exposed if that false self were not able to do this important psychic self-therapy. The splitting of the personality that is the result of this is the most important outcome of the struggle between death and survival. Clinical work with borderline adolescents demonstrates that if the false self is linked to the act of sex and opposed to the feelings associated with sexuality, and this suddenly becomes unreliable for the patient, suicide remains the only road to take. For the analyst, it may be only too easy to become angered by the patient's obligingness and treat such aspects harshly (either moralistically or intellectually), as might be the case if the patient were just neurotic, capable of distinguishing self from non-self, and therefore in some respects a whole person.

6.   From a technical point of view, the patient's vital energy manifests itself by passing from subject to object at brief moments in the relationship. The possibility of maintaining its original transitional potential depends on a technique organized around supporting these processes in the "here-and-now" rather than offering any reconstruction of them. Intermediate space is brought into being not only through the work of the subject, but through the fact that the object shares and participates in the pleasure of the pre-logical union of subject with object (Milner, 1952).

   The task of the therapist, therefore, is to allow the concrete bodily experiences of our patients to be elaborated in psychic fantasies by providing them with an intermediate space to play them out. This space can be preparatory to the ability to establish an intimate sexual space with another and is what Khan (1979) describes as "private space, separated from the social gaze, that allows symbolisms and personal rituals to be lived, learnt and taught" (p. 19). This intermediate space supports human interrelations in exchanges of trust and mutuality. Otherwise, if these defensive modalities are not scrutinized, heterosexuality will too easily be mistaken for health.

CHAPTER EIGHT

Working with women in an NHS outpatient clinic for sexual dysfunction

Maggie Schaedel

maggie and milly and molly and may
went down to the sea (to play one day)

and maggie discovered a shell that sang
so sweetly she couldn't remember her troubles, and

milly befriended a stranded star
whose rays five languid fingers were;

and molly was chased by a horrible thing
which raced sideways while blowing bubbles; and

may came home with a smooth round stone
as small as a world and as large as alone.

For whatever we lose (like a you or a me)
it's always ourselves we find in the sea

E. E. Cummings

Many women suffer from and seek to resolve the riddles of sexual disappointment. For some, the profound and distressing nature of sexual anxieties involves a referral for treatment. Current estimates vary, and a discussion in the

British Medical Journal (Moynihan, 2003) challenges the claim that 43% of women are in this situation. Clearly, a significant population of women is affected. I have worked for twenty years as a psychotherapist within the NHS, a decade of which was spent in a district service for sexual dysfunction, within the psychiatric division of a large district-hospital-based trust in the south-east of England. I assessed women from six decades of life, all of whom were deeply distressed by the absence of interest in sexual intimacy. Some complained of an indifference to sex and renounced it altogether. Others, following a traumatic experience such as childbirth, became overwhelmed with disgust. Still others remained virgins into their thirties, sometimes after many years of marriage.

"I would rather have a good cup of tea" was a phrase repeated with predictable regularity by many of these women. Some described revulsion at their own or their lover's body fluids. For others, a persistent failure of physiological arousal meant that during sex they did not lubricate, the vagina did not expand, and there was no formation of an orgasmic platform. Some women suffered from vaginismus, in which an involuntary spasm of the muscles surrounding the vaginal entrance occurred whenever penetration was attempted.

Alternative treatment modalities, including behavioural, cognitive, or couple therapies, were sometimes undertaken without success. Women continued to yearn for sexual intimacy while feeling increasingly isolated within their relationships. "My husband is very good at sex," said one who felt cheated, "but there is nothing *between* us." For all of them, sex remained at the heart of their preoccupations. They repeatedly expressed intense regret and were profoundly distressed, sometimes suicidally so, by the absence of meaningful, passionate sexuality.

During this time, I accounted for the complex aetiology of sexual dysfunction in the light of some of the insights of psychoanalytic theory. In his theory of the Oedipus complex (1923b, 1924d) Freud outlined the conflicts of genitality, the impact of the discovery of sexual difference, generational differences, and the conflict between the desire for, and identification with, the object (1920g, 1926d). The uniquely feminine characteristics for girls of this triangulated situation were not fully recognized by Freud, and the centrality and the ambivalence of the mother–daughter relationship have been widely discussed since.

The legacy of the homoerotic bond as significant to anxieties underlying sexual inhibitions is discussed by Joyce McDougall (1995), who emphasizes conflicts and anxieties in relation to the erotogenetic body of early infancy, and the universality of the bisexual and incestuous wishes of childhood. She posits the existence of archaic pregenital sexuality in which there is a struggle with the object, both real and imagined, and with inner and external realities of perceived or imagined transgressions. Elsewhere, McDougall (1990) discusses the lack of symbolic realization and affective expression as aetiological in the development of psychosomatic and sexual pathology. She suggests that sexual dynamics can become invested with existential terrors and that annihilation anxieties are axiomatic to sexual compulsions where confirmation of existence and identity is sought.

Robert Stoller (1985) discusses the significance of imagination and core fantasy to sexual excitement, suggesting the reversal of trauma to triumph as a critical component. Both he and McDougall (1995) define human sexuality as inherently traumatic.

Green (2000) describes the multiplicity of the psycho-biological components of sexuality as an *erotic chain* possessed of intricately interconnected, imaginatively elaborated links. Green (2000), Ogden (1989), and Bollas (1999) use the theory of the transitional object (Winnicott, 1971g) to describe the paradoxes of transitional oedipal configurations, where first experiences of triadic relationships develop. Within the first two-person, mother–daughter dyad, a transition is negotiated by the child between objects and experiences of internal and external significance. The infant is allowed illusions of control by a holding mother who is secure and intact, and who becomes subsequently created by the child as the first object of excited passion (Winnicott, 1963a).

Winnicott's ideas about primitive emotional development are relevant for those women who suffer intensely anxious sexual preoccupations or withdraw altogether. According to him, the aetiology of psychotic anxiety originates in the earliest mother–infant relationship. If the mother cannot achieve a state of primary maternal preoccupation, is unable to empathize and to give ego-support, then certain pathologies may result (Winnicott, 1960). A crisis may result when false-self defences break down in later life and psychotic defences, used to protect the core self, become mobilized. Winnicott describes as unthinkable anxieties, *going to pieces, falling forever, depersonalization,* and *the loss of orientation,* and these are discernible in the dissociative states to which women may withdraw when overwhelmed with sexual anxiety. When early terrors become revived and represented in the massive defensive retreat of sexual dysfunction, the capacity for intimacy in adult life becomes significantly prejudiced. There appears to have been a developmental failure to negotiate adequately the boundaries of a self-sufficing, self-soothing, auto-erotic enclave. Winnicott (1971g, 1971h) describes the infant's negotiation of the transition from auto-erotism to the excited and actual use of others. Through an instinctually linked developmental sequence, object-use evolves and the subject discovers that self and other survive what is experienced as the destructive transgressions of a passionate encounter. He emphasizes the role of illusion as critical to the infant's imaginative development of psychosomatic integration and triangulated relationship.

In describing the threat to playing imposed by ruthlessness and body-based excitements, Winnicott (1971d) states: "in seduction some external agency exploits the child's instincts and helps to annihilate the child's sense of existing as an autonomous unit, making playing impossible" (p. 52). Unconscionable anxiety or confusions result when belief in the continuity of existence, critical to the capacity to be alone (Winnicott, 1958a), is not established. Being alone carries with it the sense of another's (mother's) presence.

Winnicott does not write much about the role of the father, nor about sex, although he regards the Oedipus complex, or its resolution, as the "basis for health". From Tagore's phrase "*On the sea-shore of endless worlds, children play*", he pictures the baby as both the subject and object of creative intimacy: "The sea and the shore represented endless intercourse between man and woman, and the child emerged from this union to have a brief moment before becoming in turn an adult or a parent. . . . the sea is the mother, and onto the seashore the child is born"(Winnicott, 1971b, p. 95). In charting the development of self from the early absolute dependence within a maternal dyad and towards independence in transitional space, he proposes the evolution of a symbolizing, playful, triangulated context where instinctual life can be explored.

Where an insecure self leads to the failure to negotiate transitional space, later sexual intimacy may provoke anxiety. A fragile self may fear sex as a transgressive violation or may experience aspects of the characteristic merging of sexual ecstasy as annihilation. These anxieties may be represented in adult life in the persecutory aspects of various sexual symptoms that to the patient are both reassuring and problematic.

I have brought these perspectives to bear upon my work with women for whom sexual conflicts and anxieties become the site of clinical attention. An array of causative factors results in the common referral pathway of sexual dysfunction, a diagnosis that for some confirms the multiple trauma associated with psychic fragility.

Recurring developmental themes include the paradoxes of genitality, primal-scene and pregenital anxieties, bisexual wishes, and early developments within the mother–daughter dyad. Somatic or dissociative states point to the traumatic revival of terror and primitive anxieties in the contexts of sexual intimacy.

The resolution of an erotic impasse requires the mediation of a range of potential anxieties whose phase-associated developmental origins become inextricably interwoven. Bollas (1999, p. 160) describes the "density" of sexuality which thwarts conscious efforts at detection or description, suggesting that it is glimpsed only ever as "a fragment" and that we (psychoanalysts) "talk around it", focusing on symptoms, memories, daydreams, or erotic scenes. Within this clinical population, such fragments frequently reflected the core developmental genital anxieties of little girls, defined by Bernstein (1990) as *access, penetration, and diffusivity*. She describes the richness and range of female genital experience, which embraces urethral, anal, and vaginal sensations. Patients reported confusion when genital arousal threatened a previously established sense of body intactness. These feminine anxieties resemble Winnicott's primitive agonies that become revived in the distress of failed sexual intimacy.

That the mother of an infant's need becomes also the self-same object of the child's desire is a human paradox with which these women struggle. The position and role of a father who is repre-sented as intrusive or irrelevant is also a constant feature of the transferences of woman who are desperate for a sexual resolution.

The practitioners working in this clinic struggled with parallel anxieties. In supervisions, penetration anxiety was reflected in clinical caution and a wariness about being too direct. Narcissistic desires were manifested in the dynamics of working practices and hospital management. Tensions arose between managers and the clinicians, who felt pressured to reduce waiting lists, and targets were experienced as intrusions, threatening the clinical objectives of psychotherapy. Clinicians were charged with having accorded special status to patients whose treatments were intensified in frequency and increased in duration. It was impossible to clarify which of the complex institutional dynamics stemmed from the intricate weave of parallel processes and counter-identifications reflecting the regressive pathology of sexual dysfunction. Occa-sionally occupying the waiting-room, the mothers of adult patients would sit as sentries on guard. Whether protective or possessive, envious or encouraging, the desires and dangers associated with relational intimacy were represented within the culture of the clinic.

"A joy to be hidden but a disaster not to be found" (Winnicott, 1963a)

In treatment, these patients fend off access to their inner worlds, often regarding attempts to engage as unwelcome penetration, equivalent to the need to protect and preserve a self whose loss or betrayal is feared as imminent. Sex-refusers sought to avoid the concurrence of traumatic isolation and the desire for change within a hide-and-seek dynamic of resistance and reciprocity. Winnicott (1963a) suggests that the "most important experience in relation to the good or potentially satisfying object is the refusal of it. The refusal is part of the process of creating it . . ." (p. 182). He contends that *"each individual is an isolate, permanently non-communicating, permanently unknown, in fact unfound"* (p. 187) and espouses his central thesis, the need to protect and preserve the isolation of the self's core. Sex-refusal as a signal of distress can be a desperate enactment that confirms identity, preserves isolation, and fends off violation, but it may also represent hesitation, the precursor to playing within the paradigms of intimacy.

Patients' descriptions of failed sexual scenarios abounded with failures in self-revelation, in openness, and in the capacity to play. Winnicott (1971d) describes "playing" as both creative and dangerous, challenging the players to deal with "the precarious borderline between the subjective and that which can be objectively perceived" (p. 52). He describes psychotherapy as taking place in the overlap of "two people playing together" and free association as an invitation to a particular kind of play. That this has sexual parallels is taken up by Green (2000) who argues that the full significance of sexuality and genitality exposes the patient to the risk of having to admit the object as different from the image projected onto it. The precariousness of play, and the dynamic challenges of transitional space, are clear within the cases I now describe. In these two women, the apparent abandonment of sex and the attempted destruction of sexuality represented a failure to resolve conflicts of intimacy whose origins lay in the primitive anxieties that were revived after significant trauma. I draw conclusions from each treatment regarding the aetiology of sexual inhibition and the significance of identifying the dynamics and tensions within clinical encounters.

Marie

Marie was a pretty woman of 35 who looked ten years younger. She came to her assessment toddling on high heels, and exposed her lacy knickers as she sat down. She was warm and coquettish and showing off her exquisitely feminine accoutrements. Her doctor's referral indicated that she suffered from vaginismus, had never had intercourse, had been married for fifteen years, and wanted a baby. In the following months we explored the diverse ways in which she disguised her sensitivity and intelligence by presenting herself as a somewhat stupid woman whose surface concerns and preoccupations precluded the idea of internal depth.

Marie's early adaptation to mother had included an adhesive identification with her femininity and her anguish at ageing. Now

Marie's continued adaptive mimicry was of a mother who appeared bright and alive. But this was an *imagined* symbiotic femininity, and nothing seemed to fit. The cost to her self-identity appeared cosmetically etched on her face in clumsy traces of clown-like traumatic sorrow.

As a child, Marie had suffered from chronic constipation and obesity, and her body was frequently at the centre of her mother's and doctors' attentions. Disintegration anxiety and fears of faecal explosion led Marie to hold on to her faeces as though to her own vital somatic existence. A further loss of reality underlay her childhood conviction that her obesity guaranteed invisibility to her self. This was now further invested in her fears of violation, and the vaginismus seemed treasured as a form of self-protection.

Marie remembered feeling possessed by anxiety whenever parental noises at night signalled sex. Her father, an alcoholic, was frequently absent, or, when present, sleepy and drunk. When roused he was either angry or pathetically incompetent. She shared her parent's bedroom until she was 4, and associations and memories still held raw terror. It was unclear whether she had imagined or remembered a primal scene. She did not know whether her father was drunk with passion or with alcohol but was convinced that her mother could not bear him. A collusive rejection of this man had developed between Marie and her mother, for whom the value of the paternal function was limited to a necessary nuisance in the grand scheme of maternal insemination. Marie's mother was a socially isolated woman and remembered her daughter as a perfect baby, one rarely heard to cry or to complain, a "real sweetie". Marie had enlivened this mother with her sweetness and child-like charm..

At assessment Marie wanted me to think she was pristine. She explained she wanted sex for procreation rather than the pleasures of intimacy. She was anorgasmic, and used auto-erotic manoeuvres to reduce frustration. Rubbing her clitoris against the rough seams of underwear or palpating hard faecal plugs were secrets of a hidden private body-self whose excitements and reassurances, however, contained no tactile knowledge of her genitals.

Marie's desperation to become pregnant was born of a wish for a magical maternal symbiosis of her own, where her lack of heterosexual intimacy, her mother's ageing, and her own aloneness would be denied. A baby might solve the riddle from which as a child she could not free herself: *how does the baby get in and out of the mother's insides?* She now knew the "science" but still remembered how this mystery of creation had perplexed her quite obsessively.

At her first period, aged 13, her mother failed forcibly to insert a tampon into her vagina. Ever since, Marie had been unable to explore her genitals and had never discovered internal vaginal sensations. She rarely engaged in genital foreplay with her husband, and she suffered throughout her adult life from an acute fear of the disaster, the unendurable pain of genital penetration. Bernstein (1990) writes of a clinical phenomenon where the hymen is thought of as a sealing skin behind the labia which guards against flooding, dropping, or falling. For this patient, menstruation and vaginal secretions did not challenge her wish for autonomy and intactness.

The transformation of libido from clitoral to vaginal is discussed by Grunberger (1985) as consequent upon the psychological move from auto-erotic towards object-related experience. Identified in Marie's sexual symptom was a mother–baby dyad. For her, the body-based experiences paralleled the auto-sensuous, adhesive erotic partnership of a mother–infant couple. As she grew up, awareness of otherness, of the real differences of identity or generation, continued to be disavowed. An encapsulated feminine enclave, evolved and shared between Marie and her mother, aimed to deny time, age, and disappointments. But she also retained a hidden longing to know her father and to seek out the ordinary pleasures of the external world.

The tampon incident had confirmed the inadequacy of maternal holding, as Marie had experienced her mother as enviously thrusting the "otherness" of her own ambition into her. But mother penetrated a vagina that had no affective existence, in a painful manoeuvre that denied separateness. This traumatic rupture of the mother–daughter dyad left a legacy of confusion, hate, and revenge, hidden behind a veneer of compliance. Marie said she had learned what "raw hate" felt like and described how betrayed she had felt by her mother's ruthless attempt to possess her. She had determined to *escape* into marriage as soon as possible to avenge this betrayal. Her childlessness then aimed to deny her mother ultimate ownership of her body and her future, while her vaginismus forbade both self-betrayal and loss of intactness. Mutual masturbation masqueraded within her sex-life as intimacy, as apparent *compliance* and actual *refusal* governed all significant relationships and became interchangeably translated between her mother, her husband, and later her psychotherapist. Marie attempted to engage on the rim of a genital "hole", which represented the void that pregnancy might magically fill. She wanted to preserve body integrity, sustain symbiosis, and deny aloneness, emptiness, and grief.

The idea of the vagina as an entry point for a destructive attack, or a hole from which internal body contents might spill, is discussed by Bernstein (1990), who points out that the elasticity and lubrication that allows for the passage of a penis or a baby are unknown to the little girl for whom the vagina is passive and inert.

"Psychotherapy takes place in the overlap of two areas of playing" (Winnicott, 1971d)

Marie was trapped by psychotic anxieties and delusional body images and by conflictual desires to maintain control and overcome unbearable isolation.

Her powerfully possessive transference to her therapist offered insights into her dependency needs and desires, her identity, and her vulnerability. From the outset, she insisted on hanging around the clinic. I found her presence in the building insufferable, feeling trapped by the clamorous, persistent attentions of this patient who I felt wanted too much from me.

She had rejected mother as her *once* best-friend, but now sought protection in a feminine social reality as she tried to develop a collusive womanliness with me as an alternative to the toughness of transference. She could not reconcile the therapist on whom she depended with the one who frustrated or abandoned her between sessions. And so she tried "to get to know me", to find out what I desired.

I felt bombarded by her demands. In one session she insisted on an answer there and then, as to whether I would support her in a charity mental-health event. I said I thought she knew I would refuse, but that this might mean she could explore her desperate longing to know me more completely. Marie recoiled, curled up, rocked in her chair, sucked her fingers, and stroked her skirt. With an attempt to resort to the sensual, tactile comforts and textures of infancy, she was seeking to fill the void opened up by my words.

I wanted to acknowledge her yearning for intimacy, remain available, and enable her to confront her pain and fury. Marie considered my suggestion that she had asked me to break a boundary while knowing I would not. She often used my responses as clues to her own imagined identity, seeing what belonged to me as hers, and her failure to control or know me led her to recognize an inner emptiness and isolation. I said the therapist she wanted to know was the therapist who was now protecting her treatment as she had known I would. I had refused her friendship, she had withdrawn, and the resultant impasse reflected her sexual stalemate, where there was a failure to meet in "the overlap of two areas of playing" (Winnicott, 1971d, p. 38). Body excitements were so overwhelming (p. 52) they could never become gathered together towards an orgasmic culmination but were abandoned to the narcissistic withdrawal of sleep. Winnicott suggests that instinctual gratifications become *seductions* unless based on the capacity for play in transitional space (Winnicott, 1971b, p. 98). Marie had tried to make me hers by destroying the differences and space between us but was left with the confusions of a failed illusion (Winnicott, 1971b).

From the beginning of treatment she had nestled into hospital routines and sought to become the clinic's heroine in her self-nomination as its "sweetie". Fast becoming a "professional patient", she used the hospital culture to hide her shame and isolation. She tried to befriend other patients, conversing about anything and everything, including her vaginismus, a diagnosis she wore as a badge on her sleeve and which she used to remain on the margins of treatment.

Marie located the author of a new book on sexual problems and agreed to establish a support group, imagining that I would be proud of her. Inwardly I withdrew from another attempted "seduction", but I interpreted that she might be trying to ensure that I would hold on to her as a patient since she had failed to make me her friend. She felt ashamed and humiliated, and I feared I had been too sharp.

She then asked me to advise her about penetrating her vagina, imagining a dialogue where I would suggest she first cut her nails and insert her finger by "no more than half an inch". In weeks, she had followed these internal dictates. I wondered if this constituted an act of self-violation, a vengeful masochism, or a re-enactment of precocious intrusion. I also considered that she may now have been offering me the narcissistic seduction of having effected a cure. But I also wondered more hopefully whether she was seeking encouragement to explore her feminine sexuality from a stable parent who had held firm. Sexual intercourse followed some weeks later, without apparent trauma.

The fragile margin between seduction to oneness, adhesive identification, and true playing within transitional space had been constantly tested by Marie's intrusiveness and paralleled by her longing for a special connection, one that is also feared. The seductions of maternal symbiosis denied genitality and the shaky connection to father, but sexual intercourse had been possible and the active "non-communication" of vaginismus ended. But her need for exclusive control was exposed within the dynamics of transference, and, since her treatment goal had been achieved, she suggested I discharge her. Weeks of "audible" silences then followed. Marie had loved the sound of her voice and had derived a sense of continuity from it. Now her vulnerability seemed as palpable as the blanket of silence in which she seemed to be wrapped. Six months later, she broke off her treatment.

I was intensely affected by her leaving, and I wondered if I would see her again. I felt alone, piecing together the possible meanings of this abandoned treatment. I wondered if some aspects of the therapeutic process had been too disillusioning and how much had really changed. As head of a fragile psychotherapy service struggling for recognition, perhaps I had wished for identifiable success, so that narcissistic desires of my own may have been represented in my ongoing efforts to facilitate openness in a patient who could not play. Had Marie sensed this? The strength of this countertransference reaction was rendered less compelling through supervision where I could reflect with another and become clearer about the sources of the despair and loss I was feeling and whose feelings these were.

I had resisted Marie's efforts at seduction into the make-believe world of her erotic daydreams. It had felt both crazy and sadistic to accept these dramas passively. I had refused to be *taken in* by her, but I was left wondering whether she had taken in anything real from me. My most positive thought was that, by leaving, she was attempting to give a premature birth to her self.

A year later, Marie wrote to let me know she was well and about to give birth. I mused about visiting her in the maternity unit and then felt disconcerted at my intensely felt possessive wish to re-connect with her. Now the fantasy of transgressing professional boundaries was mine! I realized I had been waiting for her to return and again became aware of the impact of her internal world upon me.

Marie requested a re-referral to the clinic four years later. She reported some improvement in sexual intimacy and described the recent years as the most fulfilling of her life. She was aware that much had broken down in her childhood and hoped she had given her son a stronger start. But between weaning her baby at 6 months and the current impending separation of this now school-aged child, she had become overweight and anxious. She reflected on the achievements in insight and self-awareness which had transformed her relationship with her husband. She remembered those soundless, wordless sessions as potent times, when she had not felt impelled to talk to me. Although feeling alone, she had *not* chained herself to me with ceaseless chatter. In making a sex-life and a baby with her partner, she felt she had been trying to face an almost impossible choice: "*how to be isolated without having to be insulated?*" (Winnicott, 1963a, p. 187). She had been confronted with disappointment and loss in therapy where her intrusive attempts to possess me and to corrupt her treatment may have been paralleled in my unwillingness to let her go.

At four years' distance, the revival of my feelings led me to realize the intensity of identifications and counter-identifications that treating this and possibly other such patients could provoke. At times, the wish for seductive excitement that had filled Marie's internal world echoed in my countertransferences, as my capacity to reflect was overwhelmed. For a while I had lost my bearings, not recognizing my wish to rescue her from danger, pain, and disillusionment as reflecting Marie's own efforts to defend omnipotently against loss and mourning.

". . . the overlap of two areas of playing" (Winnicott, 1971d)

For Winnicott, the life of the self depends on a spontaneity originally facilitated by the good-enough mother who encourages her infant's growing needs to discover independent relationships with other people and objects. Transitional space is where the infant moves from experiences of omnipotent subjectivity in a world of magical fulfilment, to feeling able to create relationships or objects that survive in space and time. Transitional space is where illusions become realized as infants and adults work, play, and relate and where a triangulated, symbolizing relationship develops (Ogden, 1989; Winnicott, 1971g). Ego-security evolves from the self's potential to create, to bear aloneness, and to accept destructiveness. Adult sexual excitement is linked with separateness when shared between partners who surrender to desires to transgress the boundaries that separate each from the other (Stoller, 1985). Sexual intimacy develops through a wish for union that unconsciously is also a re-connection with past and present, inner and actual, realities.

Powerful dynamics are drawn into play when treating patients whose sexual difficulties inevitably involve seductive attacks. Seductions paralyse play and reflective thinking. As the exclusivity of one-ness is sought, psychotherapists may come very close to appreciating the impact of seduction on the child as it reverberates intensely within the dynamics of the adult's treatment.

Molly

Molly was a 51-year-old bank manager faced with the mid-life transitional challenges of menopause, the independence of her son, and a career plateau that would lead to retirement. She was bored at work, and her sex life was now "non-existent". Memories of a puerperal psychosis twenty-three years before underpinned a current fear of breaking down again, as did the return of obsessional symptoms that included a morbid preoccupation with her body.

At assessment she described her disappointing sex-life as a major issue and said she found herself yearning for the comforts of physical intimacy. I was reminded, as with Marie, of how separation crises can trigger sexual anxiety as partners turn to each other for intimate consolation and reunion in the face of loss. Molly described her marriage as harmonious and nurturing, but she always felt *persuaded* to "give sex" to her husband and described it as "easier if I convert it to rescuing him". The only way she could become aroused and achieve orgasm was by imagining a scene of humiliation whereby she *subjected* herself to lying face down and then *submitted* to penetration from behind. She could then surrender to a secret genital orgasm.

In the few years before her referral, Molly had presented with a range of somatic complaints including gastric disorders, chronic constipation, and mennorrhagia, but clinical investigations had produced no significant medical results.

She had been an isolated only child who grew up torn between the imprisoning deadness of her mother's routinized existence and the dangers and excitements of a relationship with a father whose manic-depressive episodes had led to several hospitalizations. Mother was depressed and passive, and Molly had sustained an illusion of self-sufficiency. Toilet-trained at 16 months, "clean and dry, day and night", she recognized that her mother's domestic obsessionality had become enshrined in her own rather rigid characterological defences. As a child, she had accepted mother's demands for compliance but through secret masturbation had found a way to manage her frustration and escape her mother. In her central masturbation fantasy, she imagined herself perched high above a classroom in a cage, watching events "down below", thus accomplishing in erotic fantasy what was never achievable in reality (McDougall, 1995; Stoller, 1985). Through the denial of her vulnerability and of mother's control, she found a way to impose her own.

Molly had felt closer to her father, remembered as warmer if explosive, but she was always anxious that he would "lose control". His most serious breakdown occurred when she was 12, and she remembered a terrifying psychotic episode that resulted in his return to hospital. She had a vivid image of her father with bulging eyes, mouth salivating, and tongue hanging out. Shocked memories of this were associated as an adult to a state of sexual arousal. She remembered when father lost control of reality and neither she nor mother felt safe. Her mother would lapse into immaturity, affecting a helpless, infantile response to him, which would drive him wilder. Sensing her mother's sadistic, mocking cruelty, Molly would try, with some success, to pacify him by talking.

Her mother had little vitality, and the dominant image was of domestic humiliation in a disastrous, loveless marriage that Molly described as a "living death". She had turned towards her father, searching for an aliveness that was only glimpsed with mother. But his aliveness was linked with manic episodes that became increasingly dangerous and terrifying.

Molly left school at 17, joined the bank, and was married at 20. She settled into domestic and office routines until the birth of her son, when she was shocked by the compulsive power of labour. Her body's momentum confused her, and her helplessness and faecal incontinence horrified and disgusted her. When she was diagnosed with puerperal depression, she coped with a programme of medication, psychotherapy, and a full-time nanny. Sex had always felt too messy, and the trauma of childbirth was complicated and messier still. But she felt that sex had produced a reassuringly healthy baby. Now, at the age of 51, the loss of her reproductive capacity led her to fear the loss of identity she had invested in her maternity and her family's intactness.

Molly's security depended on the structured world of work and family life, but loss of the family unit produced panic. She was unable to reflect, to mourn, or to imagine a hopeful future. Her body preoccupations reflected archaic existential anxieties, and, fearing sexual arousal and its associations, she had withdrawn from her husband. A strict set of rigidly determined prerequisites and conditions had previously governed this couple's sexual routines. Now she had become terrified of the uncontained madness she associated with her father and with sex. She had managed this throughout her marriage by converting anxiety into sexual excitement through an unchanging erotic fantasy that she described to me as the denouement of a thriller. Within the ordinary routines of everyday domestic life, she would feel a pulsating thud of excitement and an invisible terror that threatened to shatter her peace of mind. Her heart would race, her genital sensations intensify, and she would begin to salivate. These experiences felt real and potentially overwhelming but were contained within the temporality of a sexual cycle that concluded with the relief of orgasm.

She would describe an erotic encounter—lying awake and aware that her husband's sighing, twisting, and turning would eventually lead him to ask her for sex. She would coldly concur on condition that he wear a condom. She described her revulsion as "being a toilet for his soiling", loathing the kisses of "his mouth leaking fluid", and wincing with disgust. He would become humiliated, lose his erection, and reveal his phallic inadequacy. Molly could then react to this distress by instantly converting her disgusted fantasy of *leaking* into one of *rescuing* by manually stimulating his penis. All this time she would be in a "parallel universe" where a suited authority figure penetrated her anally from behind.

The core details never changed. Sexual excitement was generated as ice-cold disgust melted into tender care and her husband's desire turned to desperation. Her fantasy was of a powerful being who could withhold or provide satisfaction.

In the period that led to her seeking my help, Molly had felt compromised between the deadening intellectual routines of her sheltered work-life and the dread of shame and humiliation accompanying her longing for intimacy. When sexual need and arousal impacted upon her as the felt confusion of genital sensations (Bernstein, 1990), her internal body-boundaries were felt to blur. She could not continue to think and thus to hold herself together.

She became frightened, guilty, and ashamed at the destructiveness of the erotic dynamic. When her fantasy world subsided after orgasm, she felt filled with self-loathing and self-disgust and now avoided sex altogether. The term "diffusivity" used to describe female genital experience (Bernstein, 1990) is redolent of a sensual exuberance, but Molly's rigid refusal blocked a feared overwhelming flood of sexual need and greed.

Stoller describes sexual excitement as providing a sense of mastery over traumatogenic experience (1985) and suggests that "existence anxiety" is embodied in the enactment of eroticized humiliation. Molly's core sexual fantasy had always contained basic elements: one partner open and expressive, the other stilled into a passive, degrading receptivity. The desperation of one or other partner was alleviated for her by the rescue fantasy. In these circumstances, she could allow an ecstatic reunion and a surrender to passion as the distance between them melted.

". . . the ultimate compliment is to be found and used" (Winnicott, 1968)

Molly had sought to enlist me in her role-based agendas of control and desire. She would arrive early, watch the clinic from the corner of the car park, and judge the timing of her entrance to the exact second, refusing the waiting-room as an enforced humiliation of her desperately needy self. She was equally rigid in her bodily movements and her expectations of me. By piecing together fragments of fantasy, Molly began to tell me her story of a caged self, disconnected but protected from reality, one that rose above the dangers of intimate contact and potential impingement. In this she resembled Winnicott's patient who had "a dissociated life while *seeming* to be playing" (1971a, p. 29). Molly's omnipotent fantasying reassured her, and its coherence afforded relief, but the subjective control upon which she insisted could not lead to play within the therapeutic relationship.

In the early phase of treatment, I understood Molly's demands for explanatory narratives as a wish for the reassurance of a story. When I failed to supply this, she became anxious and angry. She felt insulted by a therapist who, like mother, was seen as ineffectual or who failed to know or contain her. She complained that when she was facing her greatest transitional challenge since the birth of her children, she had been drawn like a fly into the web of a clinician who confused rather than comforted or cured. It was a remarkable self-image—this fly was a contemptible, physically repulsive creature but had amazing eyes that could see in all directions. Her career had depended upon a kind of obsessional, all-seeing competence, but with her son now gone, she could neither grieve nor continue in the empty routines in which she felt trapped. She had abandoned the choreographed coercion of her sex-life and was full of shame and despair.

This patient's need for control and my awareness of the psychic fragility it masked made me feel I was walking a tightrope between intrusiveness and impotence. She was always taking flight from the impact of the "here-and-now", and my efforts to encourage her to come down from her fly-on-the-wall intellectuality and join in with me were often repudiated. She watched my continued attempts to engage with her, and I felt increasingly inept. It was difficult to locate any empathy, and I, too, felt deadened and false. On some occasions when I resorted to an artificially encouraging "Mmm . . .", Molly would swoop down to humiliate me with familiar, imperious rejoinders—"I *beg* your pardon?" "Indecipherable!" "What *exactly* do you mean?" I felt trapped as the spectator of my own humiliation. The parallels with the mismatched partners of her sado-masochistic sexual fantasy were clear. Behind her demands that I become the dangerous, sadistic partner, she longed to surrender. She tried to force me to pacify and control her with penetrative insights, just as she had persuaded her doctors to conduct invasive investigations. McDougall (1990, p. 395) notices how the upsurge of emotion is often experienced as a "crazy" intrusion into the mind. Winnicott refers to raw moments of self-experience that are bearable only when the subject feels held. For Molly, arousal and excitement could be contained only within the controlling and destructive configurations of her erotic fantasy.

She had become increasingly sophisticated at distancing herself from emptiness and grief by identifying potential anatomical sites of disaster. Fantasies of risk and survival had accompanied the invasive medical scrutinies to which she systematically subjected her body. Once, with excited terror she described the muscle relaxant used in the oesophagoscopy and based on the *curare* drug as, "also used on the tips of poisoned arrows!" The story of a beleaguered self becoming freed from monstrous terror and crushing shame was exciting and familiar. When not contemptuously dismissive of me, she was rigid, formal, and sometimes silent. Her disappointments were cogently expressed, but her silence was charged with her terror and her refusal of breaking down with fear and longing or of going mad. She was terrified of transgressive damage to a body-self, or of disintegration evoked by surrender to an overpowering object. McDougall (1990, p. 441) writes of a patient for whom the recognition of being possessed of a body capable of suffering was an achievement. But for Molly, suffering had to be named, compartmentalized, and controlled, and mortal fears had underpinned an existential dilemma: "Is sex worth dying for?"

"A good-enough environmental provision in the earliest phase enables the infant to begin to exist, to have experience, to build a personal ego, to ride instincts, and to meet with all the difficulties inherent in life" (Winnicott, 1956, p. 304). Molly remained unconsciously identified and conflicted in relation to the impinging, or unavailable parents of infancy and adolescence. She had not discovered the play space necessary to overcome relationships blocked by such difficulties, and her protective orderly self could not create depth of meaning in relationships or work.

At this time she became aware of the absence of personal creativity in her work-life, and she declared: "My anchor is my work, but I have never found a way of making it mean anything." This was a powerfully felt realization, and it registered a real aliveness between us. But mostly, I was chilled by Molly's distancing, rigid formality, although I understood it as an anxious response to my invitation to openness. When I began to voice the diffuse distress present between us, I found myself stumbling with the tensions of trying to engage her. She began to melt, and I was acutely aware that I was becoming the object of her latest piteous rescue attempt. She sought to recreate the spectrum of *distance–despair–rescue–relief* by which her erotic fantasy was bound. Contact would become erotically exciting "if I convert it to a rescuing fantasy". She had watched me anxiously and then excitedly, looking for distress and degradation. When my sentences seemed to expose a pathetic weakness, her longing intensified and she tried to bridge the distance between us with seductive sound-bites and stale storylines that were controlling and predictable. Her repetitive scripting was an omnipotent, precocious talent that once had pacified her father's incoherence but now shackled and degraded her own imagination and her image of her therapist. It contrasted with the poetic, imaginative qualities of her dreams, which became the envy of her waking self. Dream images included groundbreaking tremors and exploding, orgasmic suns, and she reported them with exuberance and some anxiety. Then there was a liquid-filled baby whose body boundaries burst with explosive internal sensations. Molly associated this violent image of disintegration with her recent pre-menopausal, menstrual flooding. She recalled the nursery story of a pitiful boy, so frightened of the flood that he remained forever stuck with his finger in a dyke-hole, plugging up the whole of Holland. *Or so he believed*. Molly knew this fear. Father was always "spilling out", and mother's disgust at any incontinence had confirmed that body mess was intolerable. She had adapted with continence and refusal, dreading an uncontrollable flood of desire.

She described waking one morning from a dream whose evocation of an overwhelming erotic longing she *could not escape* all day. From a fragment she remembered a powerful urge to possess the object of her sexual hunger: *a woman had been moaning, making indecipherable noises, and had plunged to her death into the sea.* Molly awoke with a question: *"is it worth it?"* fearing the danger of drowning in desire. The noises were "death throes or maybe the *petit mort* of orgasm". "Indecipherable" had been a familiar word in her therapy, associated with her contempt for my murmuring (renamed as my "mumbling"), the "Mmms . . ." of early sessions. She had feared them as seductions that threatened her self's intactness and refused my invitations to openness, but now, between her dream-telling and my responses, "indecipherable" could be shared between us as we began to *wonder* together.

Winnicott (1971b) describes the intermediate area of experience as a potential space existing neither within nor outside the area of play. Dream-telling embodied an alive therapeutic play-space, but one also filled with excited foreboding and uncertainty. Molly had begun to explore a critical question: "Is it worth it?"

She dreamed of a transparent, Perspex block, "phallic-shaped and small enough to fit in your pocket". It contained a visible, tiny red streak, "a sort of electric charge". I suggested she wanted to feel held by me without losing her vitality. Her passionate streak, conserved within an icy control, was glimpsed in the *block* as a truth of her self's being, defying violation. Molly had begun by regarding psychotherapy as another medically invasive procedure, but the experience of *being* in therapy had evoked longing, dread, and despair. The Perspex block invited us to *see through* it, to catch a glimpse of its dangerousness and its vibrancy as a lively connection developed between us. She said the transparent block announced, "look but don't touch". I said that if she was feeling dangerously close to touching or being touched by me, she would need to feel contained in a pocket of my mind. An overwhelming psychic intensity was invested in this depersonalized, dreamed object. Frozen, hard, and intact, it contained her need to survive "the charges" of sexuality, the guilt and shame of her longing for intimacy, her wish to melt, be held, and known. A vibrant life force was imagined, held in a pocket of erotic existence, its meaning shared and created between us. In later sessions, Molly's eye tic pulsed whenever she associated playfully to her block and the *charge* of sexual chemistry. Determined to understand this symptom, she found a definition in a medical dictionary: spasmodic torticollis, she said—"Torticollis means *screw*, screwed-up sex." Simultaneously sensing the comic absurdity of a joke, we burst into shared laughter. But I also felt aware of an uncensored contempt and collusive sadistic mockery within her words. I sensed the threat of a potential collision—of seduction and trauma—as the conflicts of Molly's sexuality unravelled and became more clearly interwoven in the transference.

Like Marie, the first patient discussed, Molly relied on the integrity of the psychotherapist whose role she also wished to destroy, and on the survival of this therapist who might then be used creatively (Winnicott, 1971h, p. 94). Both patients deployed the seductive techniques that had suffused their sex lives to try to coerce their therapist into depersonalizing and dehumanizing scripts. They had sought to liquidate the "otherness of the other" (Green, 2000, p. 157), to thwart, disarm, and mystify with myriad erotic negations. These dynamic configurations were apparent in moments of my patients' relationship to me when I discovered the precariousness of attempts to play. Remaining boundaried, ethical, and concerned while not losing vital responsiveness facilitates potential play space where self-discoveries—the "Aha!" moments of insight—may, for certain patients, express what Bollas (1999) refers to as the "*jouissance* specific to the sex-life of psychoanalysis" (p. 166). The mutually enlivening coexistence of illusion and reality is as fundamental to the development of relational intimacy as to the process of psychotherapy itself. Within the transferences of the women discussed, the dangers of intimacy became apparent, as

ruthless attempts at seductions to oneness or rigid defences threatened play and posed critical questions of practice and technique.

Molly now approaches a sexual encounter without feeling sick,
is no longer afraid of retirement, and her persistent medical consultations have ceased.

Maybe such modest changes merit her challenge to psychotherapy, "Is it worth it?" Shortly after her therapy ended, perhaps
as an aspect of mourning, Molly wrote to me with the poem
printed at the beginning of this chapter. Bollas (1999) writes that
the telling of sexuality within psychoanalysis derives from the
same "intelligence of form that calls the poet. A discourse not only
of the body . . . but from the same sources as sexual life, telling
works idea and affect into the structure of desire" (p. 165). The
talking cure that Molly sought was a seductive illusion that had
once embodied the discourses of her psychic survival. Now she
discovers a poem whose alliterative naming welds us playfully and
intimately into its structure. It conveys the *jouissance* of unashamed
insights, of moments of self-experience, of objects washed up from
memory and desire. The environment is a seashore's "endless
intercourse between man and woman" (Winnicott, 1971b, p. 95). At
its core is a self-experiencing being.

Note

I am grateful to my patients who have agreed that I may publish appropriately
disguised details of my work with them. This article is based on a lecture given
to The Squiggle Foundation in 1999.

CHAPTER NINE

Talking nonsense, and knowing when to stop

Adam Phillips

> Tyrants always want language and literature that is easily understood.
>
> Theodor Hacker, Notes

I want to start with two propositions and entangle them with a view to saying something about the vexed question of endings in psychoanalysis, and about what, if anything, the issue of endings in psychoanalysis has to tell us about endings elsewhere. The first proposition is that it is impossible to know the conse-quences of one's words—the spoken, the heard, and the overheard. The analyst can never predict the effect that his words will have on the so-called patient, and vice-versa. So, for example, whatever psychoanalytic training is, it can never train people to know what to say when, if knowing what to say means knowing what one's words can do for the patient. By the same token, one can be taught what to listen out for, but, by definition, one could never be prepared for the surprising, for whatever it is about someone else's words that is peculiarly evocative. Lacan was referring to this when he said that if the analyst has been properly analysed, he is more not less likely to fall in love with the patient. However well educated one is about one's unprotectedness, the words used are unpredictable in their effect. Language is to the speaker and listener what the daydream is to the dreamer, idiosyncratically enlivening. Learning to speak, learning to interpret, is never merely learning what to say. Learning to listen can only be learning—if that is the right word—to bear what listening calls up in you. It would have been better if Freud had said: speaking and listening is like dreaming in language. What is called interpretation is the dream evoked by a dream. It is impossible to know the consequences of one's words, the spoken, the heard, and the overheard.

The second proposition is—to adapt Valéry's famous remark about completing a poem—that an analysis is never finished, it is only abandoned. And in this, despite suggestions to the contrary, the so-called analytic relationship is like, or at least similar to, every other so-called relationship. The language of completion is unsuitable for what goes on between people. It is possible to know that one no longer sees someone, no longer has sex with someone; it is less possible to know whether one no longer thinks of someone. Indeed, one of the things psychoanalysis reveals is just how haunted we are, in spite of ourselves, by other selves, by bits and pieces of others. It is impossible, though, to know when or whether a relationship has ended. Or what it is for a relationship to end, rather than change. And yet the idea that a psychoanalysis must end—or, indeed, that one of the things that makes it so-called real analysis is that it is undertaken with a view to its ending by consent or decision rather than death—is more or less taken for granted (though perhaps in different ways) by both the practitioners and the recipients of the psychoanalytic opportunity. The opportunity of the psychoanalytic relationship is, for some people, precisely the opportunity of working through, as they would say, the ending of a relationship— something that rarely happens, and never happens in this special way, in ordinary life. Cure is the psychoanalytic word for the happy ending.

The assumption that a psychoanalysis must end—and, ideally, that it must end in a particular way that can be described and taught to the aspiring practitioner—is itself an assumption worth analysing and is something that both Freud and Winnicott were exercised by. If, say, there is a sense in which what we call "relationships" never end, then there is a sense in which what we call "mourning" may be, for want of a better word, unrealistic. (If it was a "How-to" book, it would be called, "How to go on having a relationship with someone who isn't there".) If, as Freud suggests, pleasure seeking or unconscious desire is unceasing, if the unconscious is timeless and without contradiction, then a capacity to bear frustration settles nothing. It is not about something ending but about something stopping. That wanting is endless, and that we have to have a sense of an ending; that desire is transgressive; that we fear loss of love, loss of the object, and castration—these are the preoccupations at the heart of psychoanalysis. Endings in the plural—endings as experiences that go on happening—are what psychoanalysis is about: frustration and taboo, murderousness, and the limits of one's life encompassed by the word "death". Endings are to psychoanalysis what full stops are to punctuation: they refer to, they arrange, a transition. Whether they are formal periods of hesitation—a resistance to going on that looks like a satisfactory place to end—always remains to be seen. One of the best things Winnicott did for psychoanalysis was to add the word "transition" to its vocabulary. And this is because of what it does to the idea of endings, to the strange notion of knowing when to stop. An analysis is never finished, it is only abandoned.

I want to suggest that what are loosely called endings in analysis should often be called something else, but that a capacity for abandon, and the abandon that is abandonment, could be one of the things we might hope to get from a psychoanalysis. Giving up, or giving up on, is better than finishing because it acknowledges limitation in a way that the sense of a good ending never can. Endings are not there to be engineered by us; they (and we) are not that kind of thing. If a good ending is other than a great piece of luck, it can only be a contrived (i.e., defensive) calculation. Endings, like so-called beginning, are risks; there is nothing to tide us over except what happens next. If an analyst was described as being good at endings, we might wonder exactly what it was that he or she was so good at.

It may be useful to think of at least some endings in psychoanalysis in terms of knowing when to stop. And to be more specific, knowing when to stop talking and knowing when to stop turning up. But what, from a psychoanalytic point of view, does knowing when to stop mean? If knowing and acting upon one's so-called knowledge are often so at odds with each other; if psychoanalysis makes us wonder, to put it mildly, who the knowing subject is; if the human subject is constituted by something unstoppable called, variously, unconscious desire, instinctual drives, lack—then how is the stopping going to happen? And even if we don't take psychoanalysis on its own terms, or at its word, the knowing-when-to-stop question turns up as one among many telling critiques of the psychoanalytic method. Is the analyst, for example, trained to know when to stop the patient associating, when to interrupt, given that association is both unpredictable in its rhythm and pace and uncircumscribable in its reach? Wittgenstein was famously struck by this in his discussion of Freud's method of dream interpretation. Freud, Wittgenstein is reported to have said,

> wants to say that whatever happens in a dream will be found to be connected with some wish which analysis can bring to light. But this procedure of free-association and so on is queer, because Freud never shows how we know where to stop— where is the right solution. Sometimes he says that the right solution, or the right analysis, is the one which satisfies the patient. Sometimes he says that the doctor knows what the right solution or analysis of the dream is, whereas the patient doesn't: the doctor can say that the patient is wrong. The reason why he calls one sort of analysis the right one does not seem to be a matter of evidence. [Wittgenstein, 1966, p. 42]

What Wittgenstein calls, wittily, "Freud's procedure of free association and so on" is, of course, a matter of putting a stop to the "and so on" of the patient's associations. How many associations are enough, and how could the analyst or the patient know whether the more telling, decisive associations lay up ahead, after the intervention that interrupted them? Clearly the phrase "an associative chain" itself jumps to conclusions about pertinence. It is likely, after all, that knowing where to stop—at least from the patient's point of view—means knowing how to keep at bay the forgotten, the forbidden, the altogether unsettling material. Knowing and stopping can too easily be re-described in psychoanalytic language as resisting. Knowing when to stop the flow (or other-wise) of associations can be, for both the analyst and the so-called patient, a mechanism of defence. A mechanism because it can have an automatic, seemingly inevitable quality; it feels right at that moment.

The queer thing that Wittgenstein is picking up on is the puz-zles and paradoxes associated with free association, and the resistances to it, as a procedure of truth-telling, of finding the right solution. "Freud never shows how we know where to stop," Wittgenstein says. But how could such a thing ever be shown? Where to stop cannot be known; it can only be tried out. And it will have been right not because the analyst could predict the effect of his intervention—that is, predict what the patient might say next—but because more valuable words will accrue from it. Knowing when to stop the associating makes no more sense than knowing when to stop dreaming, or knowing when to stop making slips.

The idea of knowing when to stop implies, perhaps, more coherence, more narrative structure than is always available. We say that novels and pieces of music and films end, but not paint-ings; the painter finishes her painting, but that is not what the viewer does. The viewer walks away, abandons the picture, and may return to it. Winnicott suggests that for some people, some-times, "free-association that reveals a coherent theme is already affected by anxiety, and the cohesion of ideas is a defence organiza-tion" (1971c, pp. 55–56). The patient's presenting or revealing a coherent theme, and, presumably, the analyst interpreting a coher-ent theme in the associations, is a defence. The analyst's need to find, to articulate, a coherent theme, Winnicott intimates, may also be a defence organization. Psychoanalytic theory, we should re-member, is always the presentation of a coherent theme. Knowing when to stop, in this context, means not allowing the nonsense to happen.

> Perhaps it is to be accepted that there are patients who at times need the therapist to note the nonsense that belongs to the mental state of the individual at rest without the need even for the patient to communicate this nonsense, that is to say, with-out the need even for the patient to communicate this non-sense, that is to say, without the need for the patient to organize

ense. Organized nonsense is already a defence, just as
nized chaos is a denial of chaos. The therapist who cannot
..... this communication becomes engaged in a futile attempt
to find some organization in the nonsense, as a result of which
the patient leaves the nonsense area because of hopelessness
about communicating nonsense. An opportunity for rest has
been missed because of the therapist's need to find sense where
nonsense is. [Winnicott, 1971c, p. 56]

An opportunity for rest has been missed, Winnicott says; and it is
rest from the vigilant self-holding that coherence involves. It
should not be missed that in this passage (and elsewhere),
Winnicott is describing both a new need of the individual, the need
to speak the nonsense that he is, the need for his incoherence to be
accepted as such by another person; with the implication that,
sometimes at least, our coherence is a front (and an affront to
ourselves), including, of course, theories of psychoanalysis, such as
Winnicott's. He is also describing a new kind of person. Winnicott
is always careful on these writing occasions to stress that he is
talking about a certain kind of patient or a patient at a certain kind
of time in the treatment.

For him, it is the environmental deprivation that necessitates
the vigilant self-holding of coherent narrative. The patient, let us
say, as a child had recurring experiences of having to know when
to stop forgetting himself; he was absorbed in whatever he was
doing, and this was interrupted, periodically, by a bout of need,
either his own need (the need for the object) or the object's need for
him. The problem of need, the problem of demand, for Winnicott is
that in his view it over-organizes the individual. There is the chaos
born of need that misfires because the object is unable to respond
adequately. Ideally, in what Winnicott calls "the full course of the
experience", the appetite experience has a more or less coherent
narrative. There is dawning appetite, the breast is hallucinated, the
hallucination fails to work, and the baby cries, at which point a
good-enough mother turns up, hungry to be eaten. For Winnicott,
it is not about knowing when to stop, because, if all goes well, the
process, as he calls it, has an in-built conclusion. Knowing when to
stop in this picture could only equal inhibition about damaging the
mother through appetite, or using the mind to control the process.
Here, the individual has to make himself coherent against the

problem of appetite; appetite is only chaotic, is only made chaotic, in Winnicott's view, by the object's insufficiency. Appetite will be a good story for you if you are lucky enough to have the right mother.

But what Winnicott is most interestingly attentive to is the ways in which the demand of the object over-organizes the individual by organizing at all. Winnicott is, I think, the first analyst who wanted to let the nonsense speak, as opposed to letting unconscious desire speak through free association. There are, Winnicott seems to be saying, very good psychoanalytic stories—oedipal and pre-oedipal—about the hazards of desire, and the consequent necessities of conflict defence and symptomatology. There is clearly, he acknowledges, a desiring subject as described by Freud and Klein. But there is also an incoherent, chaotic, nonsensical subject, described by no one in psychoanalysis but suggested by the idea, the method, of free association, but free association listened to in a certain way. This is the person Winnicott wants to introduce us too. The chaotic person who needs, however temporarily, to speak nothing but his own nonsense. Winnicott finds it extremely difficult to marry, or even link, the nonsensical person with the desiring person. (His useful distinction between disintegration and unintegration is an attempt at this.) The desiring person, as he develops, is always involved, one way or another, in having to know when to stop. But knowing when to stop is the enemy of chaos, or it is the omnipotent delusion that chaos can be under control. Perhaps, Winnicott intimates, what we most need to defend ourselves against, what we most believe needs to be stopped, is not the appetite—or only the appetite—but the nonsense. And nonsense can only be stopped by making sense. Why, he asks us to wonder—but in a psychoanalytic context and language—can't we let the nonsense be? Why couldn't an aim of analysis be to enable the patient to speak and bear, and even enjoy, his nonsense? And, indeed, to be able to hear the nonsense of others?

Winnicott, it should be noted, refers very infrequently to free association. He quotes with approval, indeed italicizes, Berta Bornstein's comment in her 1951 paper "On Latency": "*Free association is experienced by the child as a particular threat to his ego organisation*" (Winnicott, 1958b, p. 120). Indeed, it seems as if for Winnicott play is the word for the kind of free association that need not be a threat to ego organization. And play, of course, is not exclusively verbal. In a paper dated 1954 (but not published until 1989), Winnicott reports on a supervision:

> After the interpretation given by the student the patient leaned over and rearranged the mat and gave associations to this bit of play. In the circumstances it is understandable that the student neglected to continue on the subject of play and became bogged down in the material of the free-associations which indeed were important on their own account. [1954b, p. 28]

Clearly getting "bogged down in the material of the free-associations" is to be doing psychoanalysis as traditionally taught, but for Winnicott, in this example, that is to miss the point, which is the play. So there is free association, which, in latency, and not only in latency, is a threat to ego organization, and there is play, which for Winnicott is famously the aim, the means, and the definition of psychotherapy:

> Psychotherapy takes place in the overlap of two areas of playing, that of the patient and that of the therapist. Psychotherapy has to do with two people playing together. The corollary of this is that where playing is not possible then the work done by the therapist is directed towards bringing the patient from a state of not being able to play into a state of being able to play. [1971d, p. 38]

Winnicott here has redescribed the so-called golden rule of free association in terms of play, thereby de-emphasizing, in practice and through analogy, Freud's privileging of the verbal and the necessity of teasing out the unconscious desire being kept at bay. And somewhere between free association and play there is nonsense, which is verbal, but not exactly to be played with so much as to be accepted as such. If free association is supposed to reveal the unconscious logic of desire, playing, for Winnicott, is something quite different. "Bodily excitement in erotogenic zones", he writes, "constantly threatens playing, and therefore threatens the child's sense of existing as a person. The instincts are the main threat to play as to the ego" (1971d, p. 52). The instincts, in Winnicott's counter-Freudian story, are a threat, a word used three times in the sentence; and what they threaten is the child's "sense of existing as a person". Once again it is about sense, and once again Winnicott's phrasing might make us wonder what, if the child no longer exists as a person, he will have a sense of existing as. This takes us straight. to the nonsense question and to whether, or in what sense, talking nonsense threatens a person's sense of existing as a person.

Instinct, in Winnicott's view, puts a stop to playing—and so, presumably, to psychotherapy, which is supposed to be a form of playing. Free association, in Freud's view, can lead to the wording of desire. Do we want to be able to play, or to seek sexual satisfaction, or to talk nonsense? Of course, we don't necessarily have to choose; but if we want to play or be free to talk nonsense, our psychotherapy need never end. If we are seeking sexual satisfaction, the analyst's couch won't, beyond a certain point, do the trick.

If you look up free association in the index of Marion Milner's book, *The Suppressed Madness of Sane Men,* you find: "free association—see absentmindedness in art." This is, I think, instructive. Free associating, playing, nonsense, and states of sexual desire are all, at their best, states of absent-mindedness, of self-forgetting, of abandon. The psychoanalytic question becomes—and this is bound up, as we shall see, with the notion of knowing when to stop—what might make someone stop something as potentially pleasurable as two people playing together? If you end up getting on, and the conversation is good, why stop? This is a question any child would be radically puzzled by. Freud, in his correspondence with Binswanger, refers to "one of my closest women friends", formerly a patient. Winnicott, it should be noted, does not say that psychotherapy is two people playing together: he says that "it has to do with two people playing together", and that the psychotherapy, as such, cannot begin until the patient is able to play. If psychoanalysis, in the Winnicott way, is somehow like playing—has at least, something to do with playing—then what makes playing stop? What must be acknowledged, as Winnicott does, is the difference between a set game—which has a defined beginning, middle, and end—and open-ended play. Open-ended play is open-ended play or a defence against open-endedness. This chapter is about whether the phrase "open-ended" could possibly mean anything, and in particular could mean anything in a psychoanalytic context.

Winnicott is quite explicit that it is "bodily excitement in erotogenic zones" that "constantly" threatens play, and "therefore threatens the child's sense of existing as a person". In other words, it is play that gives the child a sense of existing as a person, whereas it is instinct, which constantly threatens play, that gives the child a sense of existing as something other than a person, or as not existing at all. So it is time to drop the idea that in some sense Winnicott wasn't interested in sex, or has nothing to tell us about what Freud wanted to tell us about. Winnicott is acutely mindful of "bodily excitement in erotogenic zones" as that which is disruptive. It is defined by him as that which interrupts, that which waylays and disfigures play. Sex, to put it as crudely, as Winnicottianly as possible, is what threatens play, what constantly threatens to put a stop to it—and, of course, to put a stop to the playing that is psychotherapy. If you want to know what sexuality is, see what you are up against when you start playing. Or, indeed, notice what stops you playing. Play is sexuality in abeyance. At a certain point, one might say, the artist loses her absent-mindedness and finds herself all too mindful that she needs something, needs someone else, something the activity of painting cannot supply. And by the same token, as it were, the point of analysis, the making and breaking point, is that the analyst and the so-called patient do not have sex with each other. The analyst, in the traditional story, is the one who is supposed to know when to stop.

Just as the Freudian analyst traditionally analyses the resistances to free association, the Winnicottian analyst, in his project of enabling the patient to play, is going to analyse the obstacles to such playing as is possible; and the obstacles are, "bodily excitement in erotogenic zones". But is the aim a capacity for such excitement, or a capacity for play? How is the excited, desiring self linked, if at all, to the self that plays? And what of the version of the self that needs the "rest", as Winnicott calls it, of talking nonsense? It is essential to the whole idea of playing, Winnicott intimates, to acknowledge what playing cannot do for the self. You can't eat art. When appetite starts, playing stops. "The pleasurable element in playing carries with it", he writes, "the implication that the instinctual arousal is not excessive. . . . Playing is inherently exciting and precarious. This characteristic derives *not* from instinctual arousal . . ." (1971d, p. 52). There is a hint of equivocation here, but it is at the moments when Winnicott's language is at odds with Freud's that the text can wake us up. Playing is pleasurable because instinctual arousal is not excessive; but—or and—the pleasure in playing is that it does not derive from instinctual arousal. The threat for Winnicott is the instinctual arousal that waylays development by over-disturbing the individual's ego organization. Playing, for him, either has no instinctual pressure, or just the right amount. In one reading of Freud, that is precisely what instinctual arousal is: the threatening of ego organization, what Laplanche refers to as "the attack of the drives on the ego". For Winnicott, where instinctual arousal was, there play should be. Or, to put it another way, the best form our instinctual life can take is in play.

And yet what playing, in Winnicott's version, cannot contain— excessive arousal—might be more exactly what psychoanalysis is about. Knowing when to stop playing might be as important as knowing what stops playing. It is, perhaps, the transitions that count: how the child moves from and through playing towards appetite and satisfaction; how the adult goes from absorption to arousal and gratification (from the vertical to the horizontal). The transition, I want to suggest, involves—is through—incoherence. One kind of chaos occurs when absorption, or preoccupation, begins turning into appetite and the hope of satisfaction. The no-nonsense self cannot make that move. Wanting comes out of an incredible muddle. Life's nonsense pierces us with strange relation.

"When we scrutinize the personalities who, by self-selection, became the first generation of psychoanalysts", Anna Freud wrote in 1968, in her Freud Anniversary Lecture "Difficulties in the Path of Psychoanalysis",

> we are left in no doubt about their characteristics. They were the unconventional ones, the doubters, those who were dissatisfied with the limitations imposed on knowledge; also among them were the odd ones, the dreamers, and those who knew neurotic suffering from their own experience. This type of intake has altered decisively since psychoanalytic training has become institutionalized and appeals in this stricter form to a different type of personality. Moreover, self-selection has given way to the careful scrutiny of applicants, resulting in the exclusion of the mentally endangered, the eccentrics, the self-made, those with excessive flights of imagination, and favouring the acceptance of the sober, well-prepared ones, who are hardworking enough to wish to better their professional efficiency. (1969, p. 20).

There is a poignant nostalgia in these words, delivered in New York in that fateful year, 1968. It is, as it were, a plea for the incoherent, for the self-contradictory, for the nonsensical. We are now fairly and squarely in the age of the sober professionalized ones, the people who know all too well when to stop. Psychoanalysis as the art and science of the indeterminate is what Winnicott and what Anna Freud, in her quite different way here, are speaking up for. The unconscious and professional efficiency are uneasy bedfellows. Which brings me back to my initial propositions: the coherence and incoherence of my theme, the connection between knowing when to stop and talking nonsense. Something about which Anna Freud's wonderful repertory company of the unconventional—the doubters, the dissatisfied, the odd ones, the dreamers, the neurotics, the mentally endangered, the eccentrics, the self-made—would know a lot about.

My two propositions were that it is impossible to know the consequences of one's words—the spoken, the heard, and the overheard—and that an analysis is never finished, it is only abandoned. Both formulations are sceptical in Stanley Cavell's sense: "Our relation to the world as a whole, or to others in general is not one of knowing, where knowing construes itself as being certain" (1969, p. 45). "Scepticism", he writes, "is a function of our now illimitable desire" (p. 3). In other words, there would be a kind of madness, a kind of omniscience, in believing that it was possible to know the consequences of one's words, or to finish—in the sense of complete with any kind of certainty—an analysis. Our illimitable desire, Cavell intimates, can be displaced into an illimitable desire for certainty.

But how are we then to define, to publicize, the professional competence of the psychoanalyst—especially in the present technologically driven economic climate—if we can never be quite sure what to say or what we are saying, and if we can't know when and whether a psychoanalysis should end? How to take up Anna Freud's late challenge? Are psychoanalysts going to be selected, let alone trained? If hard work and bettering one's professional efficiency, to use her terms, are not going to be the ambition or even the aim of the aspiring psychoanalyst; if self-selecting dreamers, eccentrics, and the mentally endangered are the preferred candidates for a psychoanalytic training—what is this training going to be like? To be acceptable to such a group of people, the training would have to be unusual, as indeed the trainings of the first analysts inevitably were.

When Winnicott is speaking up for nonsense—"organized nonsense is already a defence"—and Anna Freud is promoting the "mentally endangered, the eccentrics, the self-made", they are both, in different ways and in quite different contexts, telling us that there is something valuable, from a psychoanalytic point of view, in not being impressively coherent, something about not being wholly plausible, or, in a conventional sense, intelligible, that psychoanalysis might ignore to its cost. It is as though they are asking us to wonder what we are doing when we are making sense; when, for example, we are being, or wanting to be, strong theorists or persuasive interpreters—as though we might be at our most defensive when we are at our most plausible.

Of course, the idea that we should be suspicious of intelligibility is itself paradoxical. As an aesthetic principle, it is perhaps best captured in the poet John Ashbery's remark that "the worse your art is the easier it is to talk about". This might translate as: "the more defensive you are the more plausible you will seem to yourself." This, of course, has implications for the practice and theorizing of psychoanalysis. Making the case for nonsense, like making the case against "the sober ones, well-prepared ones", at least in a psychoanalytic context, allows us our dismay about making sense, while making us wonder where in psychoanalysis we can find now the intoxicated and the unprepared. It would be silly to take this too literally, but it would be sillier to ignore what was at stake for both Winnicott and Anna Freud in taking the positions that they did. They bear witness to the fact that, after Freud, we are awkward about our reasonableness. And our reasonableness seems to depend on our talking sense, and knowing when to stop.

If psychoanalysis has made us reconsider our beginnings—indeed, the whole notion of our origins as human subjects and objects—it has also, by the same token, revised our sense of endings. When I suggested at the beginning of this chapter that an analysis is never finished it is abandoned, I wanted to draw attention to relationships as by definition incomplete, and uncompletable. Another way of saying this would be that the ways we talk about finishing things, or about things coming to an end in other areas of our lives, are peculiarly unsuited to the ways we talk about so-called relationships ending. As readers we know where the poem on the page ends, and we know when the ironing is finished, when we have done our homework, when the football stops at the final whistle. Of course, the poem may linger in our minds after we have read it; we may find ourselves thinking or talking about the football afterwards. But there has been an official, an agreed-upon end that is recognizable. I think the formal ending of relationships bears only a superficial resemblance to these examples. A psychoanalysis ends, officially, when either the analyst or the patient decides, for whatever reason, to stop, or when the two parties agree to stop. But the question is, what is knowing when to stop knowing about? Knowing when to stop a football match means knowing about the rules of football; knowing when to stop reading a poem means knowing about the conventions of poetry; knowing when you've finished the ironing means seeing what's in front of your eyes.

There are no comparable conventions or perceptions available in knowing when to stop a relationship, unless, of course, you have prepared criteria for what it is for a relationship to end. And yet, relationships do end, in the sense that people stop doing certain things together. In professional relationships at their most pragmatic, the relationship ends when the problem is solved. And this is clearly one reason why the concept of cure has been so important, and so contentious, in psychoanalysis. It makes perfect sense, using a quasi-medical analogy, that the patient and the analyst stop seeing each other when the patient is cured. Knowing when to stop means feeling cured; knowing about people in a cured state, so to speak. But what of the afterlife of relationships, which is as real in its own way as is the life of relationships? And yet, as everyone knows who likes the sound of psychoanalysis, it is not solely or simply a problem-solving exercise. For some people, the relationship can end when the presenting problem has been solved. It is a kind of common sense that if you go to a psychoanalyst with claustrophobia, your involvement with the analyst will finish either when you are no longer claustrophobic or when you have finally given up hope of ever being changed by this kind of therapy. But you may also find, given a psychoanalytic opportunity, that whether or not you get symptom relief, you may want to go on; you may even come to believe that symptom relief may not be the be-all and end-all of the process. Not suffering matters, but not living as well as you can may matter more, and that is likely to involve suffering. Indeed, when Freud was offering us the prospect of transforming hysterical misery into ordinary human unhappiness, he was offering us a better life in terms of a better form of suffering. In other words, knowing when to stop should mean knowing what's good or you; and so, by the same token, the analyst knowing when the patient should stop means that the analyst knows what's best for the patient. My knowing what's good for me, and someone else's knowing what's good for me can be the difference that makes all the difference.

Everything we do in psychoanalysis is a version of knowing what's good for someone; agreeing to begin the therapy, intervening (or not) in the patient's associative flow, not giving advice or giving it, and, of course, finishing the analysis. There are the generalizations of theory—in Winnicott's view, say, being able to play is good for people; in Freud and Ferenczi's view, being able to free-associate is good for people—and there is the singularity of the individual analyst and the individual patient. And as everyone knows, singularity and theory are uneasy bedfellows. There is, as it were, the order, the coherence, the no-nonsense of theory, and the uniqueness, the idiosyncratic singularity of the individual. "Only a true theory", the Lacanian analyst, Serge Leclaire writes, "can advance a formalization that maintains, without reducing it, the domain of singularity; the always recurring difficulty of psychoanalysis, which no institution will ever be able to resolve, derives from the fact that it is vulnerable on the one hand to the degradation of a closed systematization and, on the other, to the anarchy of intuitive processes" (Leclaire, 1998, p. 16). What Leclaire is drawing our attention to is the senses in which theory, systematization, is supposed to protect us from what he calls the "anarchy of intuitive processes". But the countervailing risk is that singularity, the individual in his personal delirium, is abandoned. In the "degradation of a closed systematization", there is no place for the individual's nonsense; and it may be, as Winnicott only intimates, that his singularity resides in his nonsense. I think we should consider the possibility that Winnicott also believed that a person is at his most compliant when he is at his most coherent, that making sense, the wish to make sense, can be a species of conformism. In promoting the potential value of incoherence Winnicott is part of an honourable and perhaps fading tradition in psychoanalysis. There have always been nonsense and no-nonsense schools of psychoanalysis.

Singularity begins where a person's intelligibility to him/herself and others breaks down. This would be one possibility. Or we might say, a person's singularity is his or her own idiosyncratic way of being coherent. Of course, how it has come about that singularity matters to people like us is a larger question with a contentious history. But psychoanalysis, if it is to be anything other than indoctrination, has to pay attention to the connections and otherwise, between the ambitions of theory and the (unconscious) projects of singularity. This chapter wants to offer up, as case studies for this particular issue, the related and unrelated notions of talking nonsense and knowing when to stop in psychoanalysis. In what sense can there be a psychoanalytic theory about knowing when to stop—that is, knowing when to stop the patient's associations to interpret, or clarify, or comment, and knowing when to stop the treatment? Could there be, for example, exemplary instances of these things, vignettes that illustrate a general point? Are there individual examples that could serve as general guidelines? If there were, could they be anything other than a consensual agreement among a group of people about what constitutes an excellent finish? We could, for example, formulate a list of the aims of psychoanalysis and see whether or not they have been achieved; we could look at all the sentences in the professional literature about interpretation, and about endings, and see what, if anything, they have in common. We could do some research into outcomes— but where would it end? How would we know, other than by agreement, when to stop our enquiries? Some things finish; some things are brought to an end; and some things finish or are brought to an end, but are discovered to be neither finished nor to have ended. Having the last word is never going to be the last word. What makes the last line of a nonsense poem the last line could never make sense. It is part of the ambition of theory to be coherent, plausible, and persuasive; knowing when to stop the associations, the analysis, the nonsense is more like what the religious would call a "species of prophecy" and the secular might call "guess-work". In psychoanalysis there is, then, the dream-work, the death-work, and the guess-work.

Knowing when to stop, whatever else it is, is always guess-work. Psychoanalytic theory about clinical technique, whatever else it is, is a more or less coherent, plausible, and persuasive account of guess-work; of why the guess-work worked, when it seemed to, and why it didn't when it didn't seem to. Whatever the analyst's decisions are informed by, whatever their prehistory, their preconditions, whatever their training, to speak or not to speak, to end the analysis or not to end the analysis, is a guessing game. Indeed, these moments of decision may be anybody's guess; they are certainly, judging by the controversy that surrounds these issues, undecided and undecidable. Psychoanalysis, at its best, tells the individual that he or she does not need a consensus in order to speak and that that sometimes involves talking nonsense and not knowing when to stop. "Life's nonsense", Wallace Stevens wrote, "pierces us with strange relation."

REFERENCES

Abram, J. (1996). *The Language of Winnicott*. London: Karnac.

Abram, J. (2000). *André Green at the Squiggle Foundation*. London: Karnac.

Aulagnier, P. (1967). Demande et identification. In: *Un interprète en quête de sens*. Paris: Payot, 1986.

Aulagnier, P. (1975). *The Violence of Interpretation*, trans. A. Sheridan. London: Brunner-Routledge, 2001. [First published as: *La violence de l'interprétation*. Paris: Presses Universitaires de France, "Le fil rouge".]

Balint, M. (1958). Three areas of the mind: Theoretical considerations. *International Journal of Psycho-Analysis, 39* (5): 328–340.

Bernstein, D. (1990). Female genital anxieties, conflicts and typical mastery modes. *International Journal of Psycho-Analysis, 71* (1): 151–167.

Bertolini, M. (1999). L'impronta e il suo destino. *Imago, 6* (3): 195–204.

Bertolini, M. (2001). Central masturbatory fantasy, fetish and transitional phenomenon. *Squiggles & Spaces, Vol. 1*. London: Whurr.

Bollas, C. (1999). *The Mystery of Things*. London: Routledge.

Bornstein, B. (1951). On latency. *Psychoanalytic Study of the Child, 6*.

Budd, S. (2001). "No sex, please—we're British": Sexuality in English and French psychoanalysis. In: C. Harding (Ed.), *Sexuality: Psycho-analytic Perspectives* (pp. 52–68). London: Routledge.

Bychowski, G. (1955). "The Release of Internal Images." Paper presented at the 19th International Psycho-Analytic Congress, Geneva.

Cavell, S. (1969). *Must We Mean What We Say?* (Modern Philosophical Essays in Morality, Religion, Drama, Music, and Criticism.) New York: Charles Scribner's Sons.

Davis, M., & Wallbridge, D. (1981). *Boundary and Space: An Introduction to the Work of D. W. Winnicott*. New York: Brunner-Mazel. [Revised edition: London: Karnac, 1991.]

Donne, J. (1633). The Good-Morrow. In: *The Complete English Poems*. London: Everyman Library, 1985.

Fairbairn, W. R. D. (1952). *Psychoanalytic Studies of the Personality*. London: Tavistock.

Ferenczi, S. (1932). *Fondamenti in psicoanalisi*. Guaraldi: Firenze.

Ferenczi, S. (1933). Confusion of tongues between adults and the child. In: *Final Contributions to Problems and Methods of Psychoanalysis*. London: Karnac, 1980. [Also published in: *International Journal of Psycho-Analysis, 30* (1949).]

Freeman, W. J. (1999). *How Brains Make up Their Mind*. London: Weidenfeld & Nicholson.

Freud, A. (1967). Fears, anxieties and phobic phenomena. *Psychoanalytic Study of the Child, 32*: 85.

Freud, A. (1969). *The Writings of Anna Freud, Vol. 7*. London: Hogarth Press.

Freud, S. (1900a). *The Interpretation of Dreams. S.E.*, 1.

Freud, S. (1905d). *Three Essays on the Theory of Sexuality. S.E.*, 7.

Freud, S. (1905e [1901]). Fragment of an analysis of a case of hysteria. *S.E.*, 7.

Freud, S. (1908e [1907]). Creative writers and day-dreaming. *S.E.*, 9.

Freud, S. (1909b). Analysis of a phobia in a five-year-old boy. *S.E.*, 10.

Freud, S. (1909d). Notes upon a case of hysterical neurosis. *S.E.*, 10.

Freud, S. (1910c). *Leonardo da Vinci and a Memory of His Childhood. S.E.*, 11.

Freud, S. (1918b [1914]). From the history of an infantile neurosis. *S.E.*, 17.

Freud, S. (1919e). A child is being beaten: A contribution to the study of the origin of sexual perversions. *S.E.*, 17.

Freud, S. (1920g). *Beyond the Pleasure Principle. S.E.*, 18.

Freud, S. (1923b). *The Ego and the Id. S.E.*, 19.

Freud, S. (1924d). The dissolution of the Oedipus complex. *S.E.*, 19.

Freud, S. (1926d [1925]). *Inhibition, Symptoms and Anxiety. S.E.*, 20.

Freud, S. (1939a [1937–39]). *Moses and Monotheism. S.E.*, 23.

Freud, S. (1940a [1938]). *An Outline of Psychoanalysis. S.E.*, 23.

Freud, S. (1950 [1892–1889]). Extracts from the Fliess Papers. *S.E. 1.*

Freud, S. (1985). *The Complete Letters of Sigmund Freud to Wilhelm Fliess 1887–1904,* trans. and ed. J. M. Masson. Cambridge, MA, & London: Harvard University Press.

Freud, S. (1990). *Epistolari: Lettere a Fliess 1887–1904.* Turin: Boringhieri.

Gaddini, E. (1984). Changes in psychoanalytic patients up to the present day. In: *A Psychoanalytic Theory of Infantile Experience: Conceptual and Clinical Reflections.* London: Routledge & The New Library of Psychoanalysis, 1992.

Gardner, H. (Ed.) (1957). *The Metaphysical Poets.* London: Penguin Classics, reprinted 1985.

Giannakoulas, A. (1988). Reflections on the relatedness between the pathology of the couple and the symptoms of the child. In: *Psicosi Infantili ed ambiente terapeutico.* Rome: Borla.

Giannakoulas, A. (1993). Clinical notes on the processes of falling in love, marriage and parenthood. *Psicobiettivo, 1* (Jan.–Apr.).

Giannakoulas, A. (1997). Corteggiamento, innamoramento, amore e genitorialità. In: A. M. Nicolò (Ed.), *Curare la relazione.* Rome: Il Pensiero Scientifico.

Gillespie, W. H. (1955). The general theory of sexual perversion. In: M. D. A. Sinason (Ed.), *Life, Sex, and Death.* London: Routledge & The New Library of Psychoanalysis, 1995. [Paper read at the 19th International Psycho-Analytic Congress, Geneva, 1955.]

Glover, E. (1945). An examination of the Klein system of child psychology. *Psychoanalytic Study of the Child, 1*: 75–118.

Gopnik, A., & Meltzoff, A. N. (1997). *Words, Thoughts and Theories.* Cambridge, MA: MIT Press.

Green, A. (1993). La mère morte. In: *Narcissisme de Vie, Narcississsme de Mort.* Paris: Minuit.

Green, A. (1997). The intuition of the negative in *Playing and Reality. International Journal of Psycho-Analysis, 78* (6): 1071–1084.

Green, A. (2000). *The Chains of Eros.* London: Karnac.

Greenacre, P. (1973). The primal scene and the sense of reality. *Psychoanalytic Quarterly*, 42: 10–41.

Greenacre, P. (1975). *Emotional Growth*. New York: International Universities Press.

Grunberger, B. (1985). Narcissism in female sexuality. In: J. Chasseguet-Smirgel (Ed.), *Female Sexuality: New Psychoanalytic Views*. London: Karnac.

Guntrip, H. (1975). My experience of analysis with Fairbairn and Winnicott. *International Journal of Psycho-Analysis, 77* (1996, No. 4): 739–754. [First published in *International Journal of Psycho-Analysis, 2* (1975): 145–156.]

Heimann, P. (1952). A contribution to the re-evaluation of the Oedipus complex: The early stages. In: *About Children and Children-No-Longer. Collected Papers 1942–80*. London & New York: Tavistock/ Routledge, 1989.

Hopkins, L. (1998). D. W. Winnicott's analysis of Masud Khan. *Contemporary Psychoanalysis, 34*: 5–8.

Hopkins, L. (2000). Masud Khan's application of Winnicott's "play" techniques to analytic consultation and treatment of adults. *Contemporary Psychoanalysis, 56*: 639–663.

Joffe, W. (1969). A critical review of the status of the envy concept. *International Journal of Psycho-Analysis, 50* (4): 533–545.

Khan, M. (1972). The use and abuse of dream in psychic experience. In: *The Privacy of the Self* (pp. 306–314). London: Hogarth Press, 1974.

Khan, M. (1979). *Alienation in Perversions*. Madison, CT: International Universities Press.

Kierkegaard, S. (1843). *Il riflesso del tragico antico nel tragico moderno in Antigone e la filosofia* (pp. 49–71). Rome: Donzelli ed., 2001.

Klein, M. (1957). *Envy and Gratitude*. London: Hogarth Press, 1975.

Kohon, G. (Ed.) (1999). *The Dead Mother: The Work of André Green*. London: Routledge & The New Library of Psychoanalysis.

Kolb, L. C., & Johnson, A. M. (1955). Etiology and therapy of overt homosexuality. *Psychoanalytic Quarterly, 24*: 506.

Laplanche, J. (1980). *Problématiques III: La sublimation*. Paris: Presses Universitaires de France.

Laplanche, J. (1987). *Nouveaux fondements pour la psychanalyse*. Paris: Presses Universitaires de France.

Laplanche, J. (1989). *New Foundations for Psychoanalysis*, trans. D. Macey. Oxford: Blackwell.

Laplanche, J. (1990). Implantation, intromission. In: *La primauté de l'autre en psychanalyse*. Paris: Flammarion, Coll. "Champs" [English edition: *Essays in Otherness*, ed. J. Fletcher London: Blackwell. 1998].

Laplanche, J. (1997). La révolution copernicienne inachevée. In: *La primauté de l'autre en psychanalyse*. Paris: Flammarion, Coll. "Champs" [English edition: *Essays in Otherness*, ed. J. Fletcher. London: Blackwell, 1998].

Laplanche, J., & Pontalis, J.-B. (1967). *Vocabulaire de la Psychanalyse*. Paris: Presses Universitaire de France. [English edition: *The Language of Psychoanalysis*. London: Hogarth Press, 1973; reprinted London: Karnac, 1988.]

Laufer, E., & Laufer, M. (1989). *Adolescence and Developmental Breakdown: A Psychoanalytic View*. New Haven, CT: Yale University Press.

Leclaire, S. (1998). *Psychoanalyzing: On the Order of the Unconscious and the Practice of the Letter*, trans. P. Kamuf. Palo Alto, CA: Stanford University Press.

Little, M. (1985). Winnicott working in areas where psychotic anxieties predominate: A personal record. *Free Associations, 3*: 9–42.

Little, M. (1987). On the value of regression to dependence. *Free Associations, 10*: 7–22.

Masciangelo, P. M. (1988). La nascita dell'aggressività: dall'esperienza psicoanalitica alla teoria. In: *La relazione aggressiva*. Rome: Borla.

Mason, M. (2000). Bion and binocular vision. *International Journal of Psycho-Analysis, 81*: 983–990.

McDougall, J. (1989). *Theatres of the Body*. London: Free Association Books.

McDougall, J. (1990). *Plea for a Measure of Abnormality*. London: Free Association Books.

McDougall, J. (1995). *The Many Faces of Eros*. London: Free Association Books.

Milner, M. (1952). The role of illusion in symbol formation. In: *The Suppressed Madness of Sane Men* (pp. 83–114). London: Tavistock, 1987.

Moynihan, R. (2003). The making of a disease: Female sexual dysfunction. *British Medical Journal, 326*: 45–47.

Newman, A. (1995). *Non-Compliance in Winnicott's Words: A Companion to the Work of D.W. Winnicott*. New York: New York University Press.

Ogden, T. H. (1989). *The Primitive Edge of Experience*. North Vale, NJ, & London: Jason Aronson.

Parsons, M. (1999). Psychic reality, negation and the analytic setting. In: G. Kohon, *The Dead Mother* (pp. 59–75). London: Routledge & The New Library of Psychoanalysis.

Payne, S. (1939). Some observations on the ego development of the fetishist. *International Journal of Psycho-Analysis, 20*.

Phillips, A. (1988). *Winnicott*. London: Fontana Press.

Pontalis, J.-B. (1977). *Frontiers in Psychoanalysis*. London: Hogarth Press and The Institute of Psycho-Analysis.

Rayner, E. (1991). *The Independent Mind in British Psychoanalysis*. London: Free Association Books.

Rilke, R. M. (1964). *Orpheus, Eurydice, Hermes*. In: *New Poems*, trans. J. B. Leishman. New York: New Directions Books.

Roustang, F. (1982). *Dire Mastery: Discipleship from Freud to Lacan*. Baltimore, MD: Johns Hopkins University Press.

Rycroft, C. (1956). Symbolism and its relationship to the primary and secondary processes. In: *Imagination and Reality* (pp. 42–60). London: Karnac, 1987.

Rycroft, C. (1987). *Imagination and Reality*. London: Karnac.

Sadger, J. (1921). *Die Lehre von den Geschlechtsverirrungen (Psychopathia Sexualis) auf Psychoanalytische Grundlage* (pp. 37–39). Vienna: Deuticke (International Psychoanalytische Vereinigung).

Scarfone, D. (1998). Machines à écrire vérités et mensonges. *Trans, 9*: 31–42.

Scarfone, D. (1999). Les trahisons nécessaires. In: D. Scarfone (Ed.), *De la trahison* (pp. 93–109). Paris: Presses Universitaires de France.

Scarfone, D. (2003). "It was *not* my mother": From seduction to negation. *New Formations, 48* (Winter 2002–2003): 69–76.

Schur, M. (1958). The ego and the id in anxiety. *Psychoanalytic Study of the Child, 13*: 190.

Spurling, L. (2002). On psychoanalytic figures as transference objects. *International Journal of Psycho-Analysis, 84* (1): 31–44.

Stoller, R. J. (1985). *Observing the Erotic Imagination*. New Haven, CT, & London: Yale University Press.

Sutherland, J. (1963). *British Journal of Psychiatric Social Work, 7* (2): 64–72.

Winnicott, D. W. (1941). The observation of infants in a set situation.

In: *Through Paediatrics to Psychoanalysis* (pp. 52–70). London: Karnac.

Winnicott, D. W. (1945). Primitive emotional development. In: *Through Paediatrics to Psychoanalysis* (pp. 145–156). London: Karnac.

Winnicott, D. W. (1951). Critical notice of *On Not Being Able to Paint*. In: *Psychoanalytic Explorations* (pp. 390–392), ed. C. Winnicott, R. Shepherd, & M. Davis. London: Karnac, 1989.

Winnicott, D. W. (1953). Transitional objects and transitional phenomena. In: *Through Paediatrics to Psycho-Analysis*. London: Hogarth Press, 1975.

Winnicott, D. W. (1954a). Metapsychological and clinical aspects of regression within the psycho-analytical setting. In: *Through Paediatrics to Psycho-Analysis*. London: Hogarth Press, 1975.

Winnicott, D. W. (1954b). Play in the analytic situation. In: *Psychoanalytic Explorations* (pp. 28–29), ed. C. Winnicott, R. Shepherd, & M. Davis. London: Karnac, 1989.

Winnicott, D. W. (1956). Primary maternal occupation. In: *Through Paediatrics to Psycho-Analysis* (pp. 300–305). London: Hogarth Press, 1975.

Winnicott, D. W. (1958a). The capacity to be alone. In: *The Maturational Processes and the Facilitating Environment* (pp. 29–36). London: Karnac, 1990.

Winnicott, D. W. (1958b). Child analysis in the latency period. In: *The Maturational Processes and the Facilitating Environment* (pp. 115–123). London: Karnac, 1990.

Winnicott, D. W. (1960). Ego distortion in terms of true and false self. In: *The Maturational Processes and the Facilitating Environment* (pp. 140–152). London: Hogarth Press.

Winnicott, D. W. (1962). A personal view of the Kleininan contribution. In: *The Maturational Processes and the Facilitating Environment* (pp. 171–178). London: Karnac, 1990.

Winnicott, D. W. (1963a). Communicating and not communicating leading to a study of certain opposites. In: *The Maturational Processes and the Facilitating Environment* (pp. 179–192). London: Karnac, 1990.

Winnicott, D. W. (1963b). Fear of breakdown. In: *Psychoanalytic Explorations* (pp. 87–95), ed. C. Winnicott, R. Shepherd, & M. Davis. London: Karnac, 1989.

Winnicott, D. W. (1966). The split-off male and female elements to be found in men and women. In: *Psychoanalytic Explorations* (pp. 169–192), ed. C. Winnicott, R. Shepherd, & M. Davis. London: Karnac, 1989.

Winnicott, D. W. (1968). The use of an object and relating through identifications. In: *Psychoanalytic Explorations* (pp. 217–227), ed. C. Winnicott, R. Shepherd, & M. Davis. London: Karnac, 1989.

Winnicott, D. W. (1971a). Dreaming, fantasying, and living: A case-history describing a primary dissociation. In: *Playing and Reality* (pp. 26–37). London: Routledge/Tavistock.

Winnicott, D. W. (1971b). The location of cultural experience. In: *Playing and Reality* (pp. 95–104). London: Routledge/Tavistock.

Winnicott, D. W. (1971c). Playing: Creative activity and the search for self. In: *Playing and Reality* (pp. 53–64). London: Routledge/Tavistock.

Winnicott, D. W. (1971d). Playing: A theoretical statement. In: *Playing and Reality* (pp. 38–52). London: Routledge/Tavistock.

Winnicott, D. W. (1971e). *Playing and Reality*. London: Routledge/Tavistock.

Winnicott, D. W. (1971f). *Therapeutic Consultations in Child Psychiatry*. London: Hogarth Press.

Winnicott, D. W. (1971g). Transitional objects and transitional phenomena. In: *Playing and Reality* (pp. 1–25). London: Routledge/Tavistock.

Winnicott, D. W. (1971h). The use of an object and relating through identifications. In: *Playing and Reality* (pp. 86–94). London: Routledge/Tavistock.

Winnicott, D. W. (1977). *The Piggle*. London: Hogarth Press.

Winnicott, D. W. (1987). *The Spontaneous Gesture*, ed. F. R. Rodman. Cambridge, MA: Harvard University Press.

Winnicott, D. W. (1988). *Human Nature*, ed. C. Bollas, M. Davis, & R. Shepherd. London: Free Association Books.

Winnicott, D. W. (1989). On "The Use of an Object". In: *Psychoanalytic Explorations* (pp. 217–247), ed. C. Winnicott, R. Shepherd, & M. Davis. London: Karnac.

Wittgenstein, L. (1966). *Lectures and Conversations on Aesthetics, Psychology and Religious Belief*. Oxford: Blackwell.

Zucconi, S. (2003). "L'amore perverso." Unpublished paper given to the Italian Psychoanalytical Association (SPI), Rome, 26 October.

INDEX